THE CHURCH BULLETIN CLIP ART BOOK

Tom Finley

We would love to receive samples of your church bulletins! Feel free to put us on your mailing list. And send us your ideas and suggestions for improving future Gospel Light Clip Art Books. We want our books to be as good as they can be! We regret that we cannot reply to all correspondence.

Address your submissions to:

Church Curriculum Services
Gospel Light Publications
2300 Knoll Dr.
Ventura, CA 93003

Appreciation for kind assistance is expressed to:

Brenda, Byron Cressy, Annette Parrish, Nina Fishwick, Rick Bundschuh, Wes and Sheryl Haystead, and all the churches which contributed valuable ideas via their bulletins.

Scripture taken from the *Holy Bible, New International Version.* Copyright © 1973, 1978, 1984 International Bible Society. Used by permission of Zondervan Bible Publishers.

Also quoted is the King James Version.

6 7 8 9 10 / 91

THE CHURCH BULLETIN CLIP ART BOOK

THE CHURCH BULLETIN CLIP ART BOOK

CONTENTS

HOW TO USE THE CHURCH BULLETIN CLIP ART BOOK

BEFORE YOU BEGIN

THE TOOLS AND SUPPLIES REQUIRED:

☐ Pencil and sharpener

☐ Eraser

☐ Scratch paper

☐ Rubber cement

☐ Ruler

☐ Scissors

☐ X-Acto knife with #11 blades

☐ Typewriter and paper

☐ Correction fluid

☐ Paper towels

☐ Non-repro blue pen or pencil. (A very light blue which "drops out" when photocopied.)

☐ Transfer (rub-on or peel-and-stick) letters and numbers

☐ Burnishing tool to apply transfer letters

☐ Cardstock for paste-up

The last four items can be purchased at any good art supply store.

DECISIONS TO BE MADE:

Place a check mark in each box as you make these important determinations.

1. What is the bulletin's size (before folding)?
   ☐ 8½″ × 11″
   ☐ 8½″ × 14″
   ☐ 11″ × 17″
   ☐ Other: _____ (May require trimming at extra cost.)

2. Printed how many sides?
   ☐ One side
   ☐ Both sides
   ☐ Both sides of multiple sheets

3. Number of copies to be printed: _____

4. Kind and color of paper: _____ (If these are being professionally printed, review sample stock at the printers.)

5. Ink (if professionally printed).
   ☐ One. Color of ink: _____
   ☐ More than one: _____

6. Date paste-up must be delivered for printing: _____

7. Date product must be mailed: _____

4

A FEW WORDS OF ADVICE:

We recommend that you print your bulletins on the finest paper you can reasonably afford. Paper and printing quality can make or break the appearance of your publication. If at all possible, avoid using a spirit duplicator!

PREPARING ARTWORK FOR PUBLICATION

Assuming you have composed the manuscript for your bulletin or other publication:

1. Prepare your paste-up sheets. These are the sheets to which you'll paste your artwork and typewritten copy. Use cardstock, thick enough to be durable and thin enough to cut with scissors or knife. You will need one sheet for each printed side of your product.

   Prepared paste-up sheets, printed with very light blue graph paper-style guide lines (which "drop out" when photocopied or printed), can be purchased at art supply stores. The sheets come in various sizes. We highly recommend their use.

   Make your paste-up sheets the same size as the final product, or slightly larger.

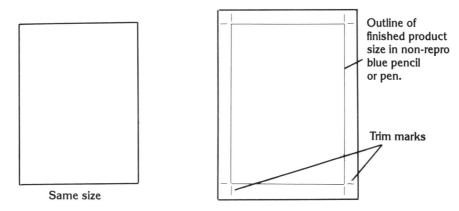

Same size

Outline of finished product size in non-repro blue pencil or pen.

Trim marks

If your bulletin folds, the pages must be pasted up in these positions:

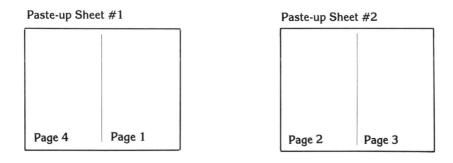

Paste-up Sheet #1

Page 4   Page 1

Paste-up Sheet #2

Page 2   Page 3

2. Locate in this book the artwork, headlines, and borders you wish to use. Clip them out as shown.

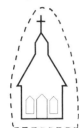  

3. Make a rough draft layout of your page design. Use your pencil and scratch paper to sketch ideas.

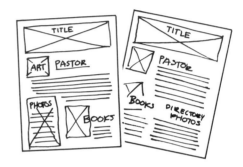

4. Now get out your trusty typewriter. Type your manuscript to fit the space your layout design allows. A good way to do this is to first outline on your typing paper the exact dimensions of the areas devoted to copy. Do this by laying the paper on your layout and tracing the areas with your non-repro pencil or pen. Then simply insert the paper into your typewriter and type within the marked outlines.

An alternate method of page layout design is this: Clip out the art you intend to use, type your manuscript in columns, cut the manuscript into small pieces (subject by subject or paragraph by paragraph), and then experiment with arrangements of art and copy.

Three tips:

You can get more on the page if you have your typewritten copy photographically reduced in size. Your local printers can provide this service.

Professional typesetting is expensive, but it dramatically improves the appearance of your product. Look in the phone book for typesetters.

Custom headlines can be constructed with rub-on or peel-and-stick letters. Very nice looking and modern type styles are available, but only at finer art supply stores. Complete instructions for use are published in the manufacturers' catalogs. The best type styles come from **Letraset** and **Formatt.**

6

5. Use rubber cement to paste your copy and art to the paste-up board. A ruler and triangle should be used to keep everything straight and aligned. (If you are using graph paper-style paste-up board, you won't need the ruler or triangle.)

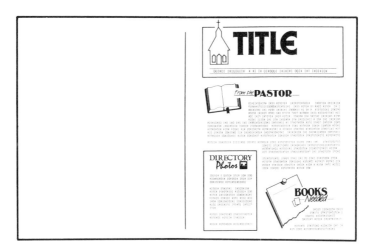

Cleanliness counts! Be sure to erase all pencil lines and remove all smudges.

6. Your job is now ready to be printed or photocopied.

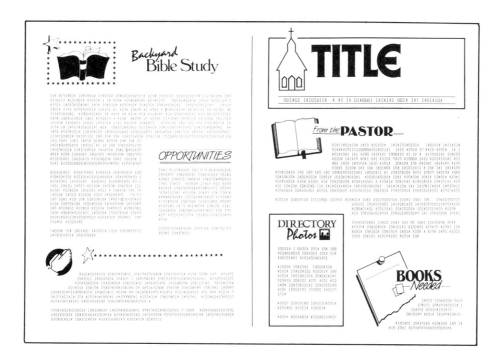

AN EXAMPLE:

Here is just one example of the wonderful results you can achieve with your creativity and this clip art book.

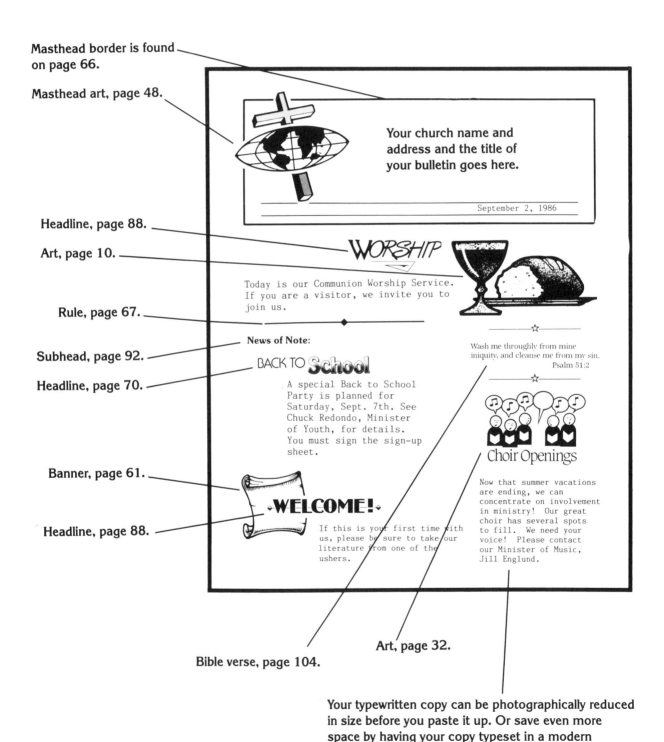

Masthead border is found on page 66.

Masthead art, page 48.

Your church name and address and the title of your bulletin goes here.

September 2, 1986

Headline, page 88.

Art, page 10.

WORSHIP

Today is our Communion Worship Service. If you are a visitor, we invite you to join us.

Rule, page 67.

News of Note:

Subhead, page 92.

BACK TO School

Headline, page 70.

A special Back to School Party is planned for Saturday, Sept. 7th. See Chuck Redondo, Minister of Youth, for details. You must sign the sign-up sheet.

Wash me throughly from mine iniquity, and cleanse me from my sin.
Psalm 51:2

Choir Openings

Banner, page 61.

WELCOME!

Headline, page 88.

If this is your first time with us, please be sure to take our literature from one of the ushers.

Now that summer vacations are ending, we can concentrate on involvement in ministry! Our great choir has several spots to fill. We need your voice! Please contact our Minister of Music, Jill Englund.

Art, page 32.

Bible verse, page 104.

Your typewritten copy can be photographically reduced in size before you paste it up. Or save even more space by having your copy typeset in a modern compact style.

CLIP ART

This section contains all the clip art you need for at least a year's worth of bulletins, handbills, newsletters, Bible study worksheets, overhead transparencies and more.

Because church bulletins often allow so little space, we have made the art as "teensy-weensy" as possible. Larger versions of each piece of art are also provided for use when your space allows.

Each page is blank on the back so artwork can be clipped out without ruining art on the reverse side.

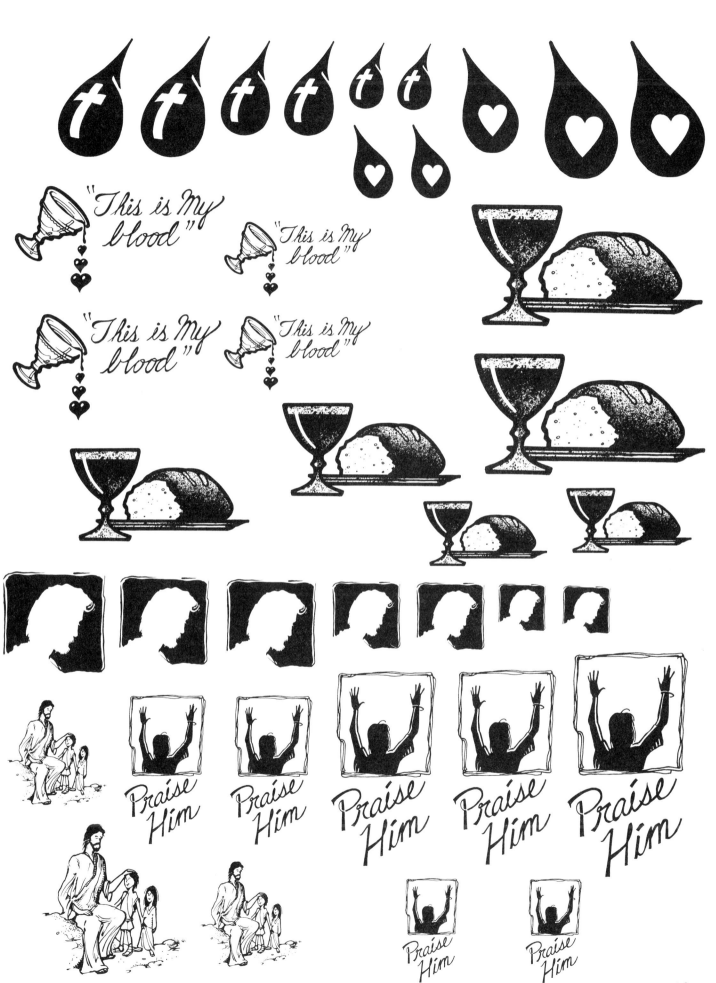

"This is My blood"

"This is My blood"

"This is My blood"

"This is My blood"

Praise Him

Praise Him

Praise Him

Praise Him

Praise Him

Praise Him

Praise Him

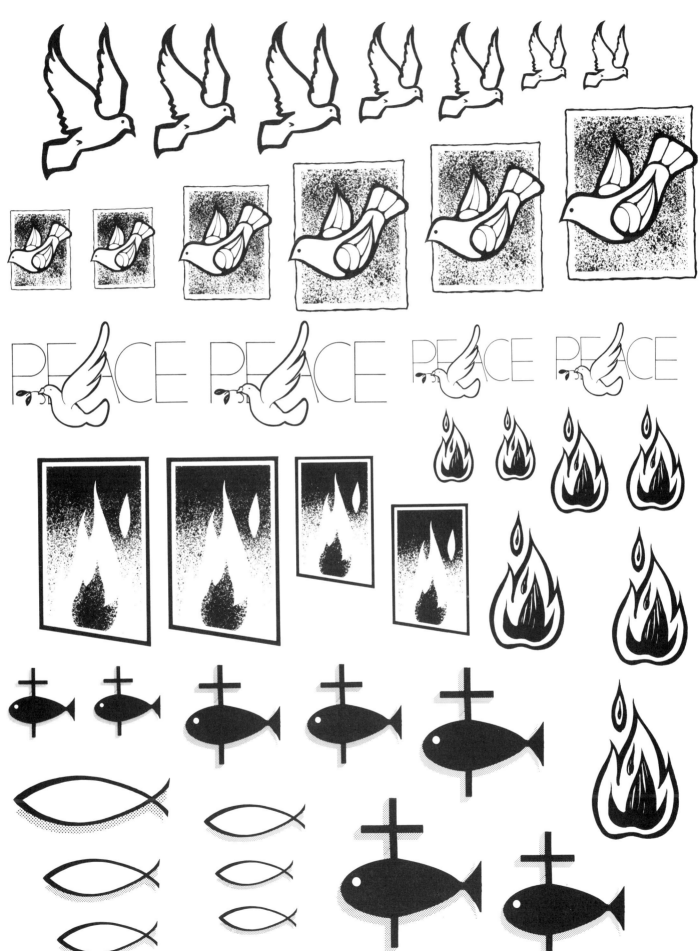

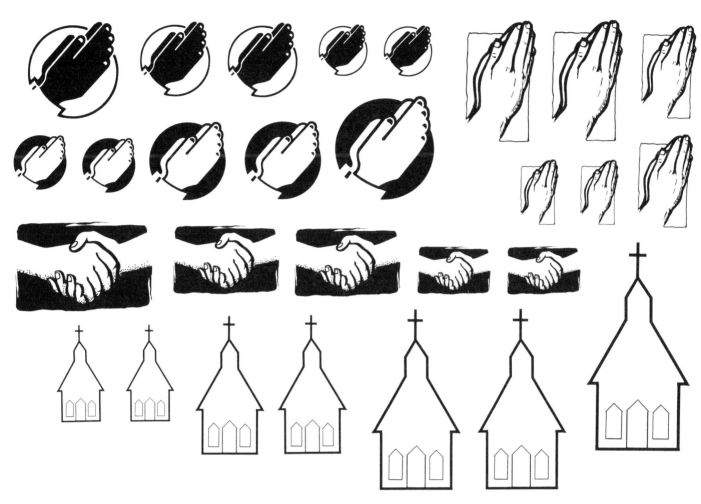

 from the Pastor's desk

 from the Pastor's desk

 from the Pastor's desk

 from the Pastor's desk

 from the Pastor's desk

 from the Pastor's desk

 from the Pastor's desk

PASTOR'S NOTES

PASTOR'S NOTES

PASTOR'S NOTES

PASTOR'S NOTES

PASTOR'S NOTES

PASTOR'S NOTES

13

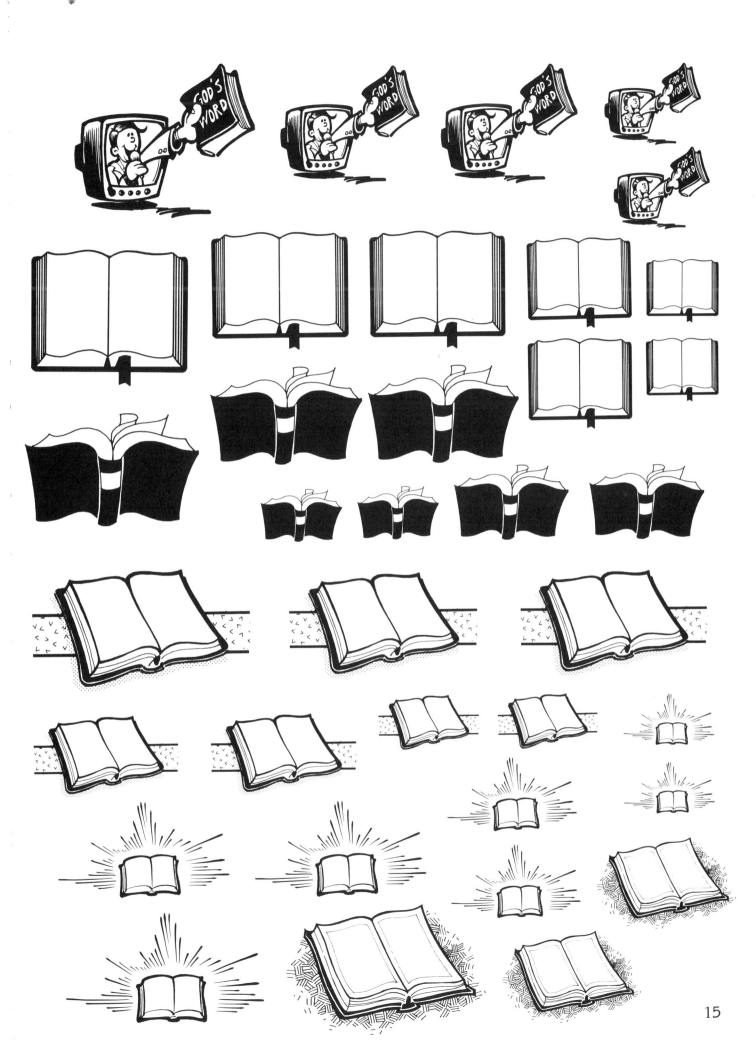

17

18

EVENTS

RETREATS AND SEMINARS

Couple's Retreat

Divorce Recovery Workshop

Divorce Recovery Workshop

Divorce Recovery Workshop

Divorce Recovery Workshop

Divorce Recovery Workshop

Divorce Recovery Workshop

Divorce Recovery Workshop

Father/son

Father/son

Father/son

Father/son

Mother-Daughter Weekend

Mother-Daughter Weekend

Mother-Daughter Weekend

PARENTING SEMINAR

Mother-Daughter Weekend

PARENTING SEMINAR

PARENTING SEMINAR

PARENTING SEMINAR

PARENTING SEMINAR

CHURCH Workday

CHURCH Workday

CHURCH Workday

Church Workday

Church Workday

Church Workday

Church Workday

Church Workday

Clothing Drive

Clothing Drive

Clothing Drive

Clothing Drive

Convention

Convention

Convention

Convention

Convention

Counseling

Counseling

Counseling

Counseling

Counseling

Famine RELIEF

Famine RELIEF

Famine RELIEF

Famine RELIEF

Famine RELIEF

Fellowship

Fellowship

Fellowship

Fellowship

Fellowship

Fellowship

Fellowship

Graduation   *Graduation*

Graduation

Graduation   *Graduation*

Jog-a-thon

Walk-a-thon

Jog-a-thon

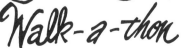
Walk-a-thon

Jog-a-thon

OPEN HOUSE

 OPEN HOUSE **OPEN HOUSE**

 OPEN HOUSE   **OPEN HOUSE**   **OPEN HOUSE**   **OPEN HOUSE**

 PAPER RECYCLE

 PAPER RECYCLE

 **PAPER RECYCLE**   **PAPER RECYCLE**

 **PAPER RECYCLE**    **PAPER RECYCLE**

 **PAPER RECYCLE**   **PAPER RECYCLE**

SPORTS _____

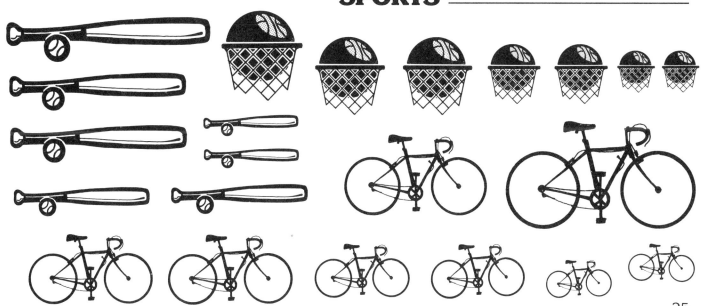

25

FOOD ——————————————————————

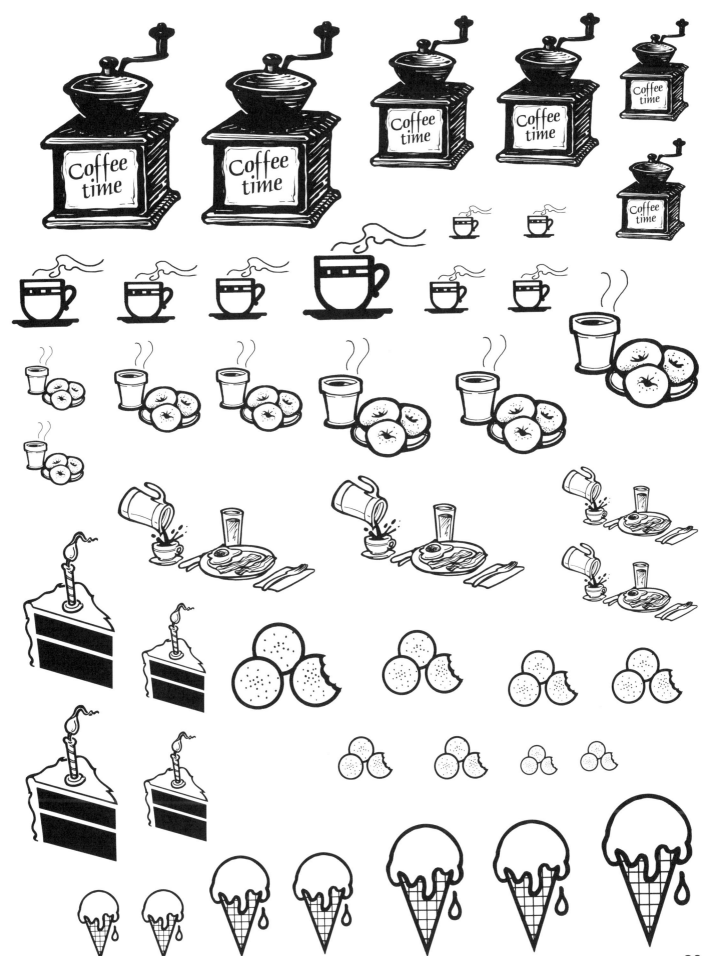

28

PROGRESSIVE DINNER

PROGRESSIVE DINNER

PROGRESSIVE DINNER

PROGRESSIVE DINNER

PROGRESSIVE DINNER

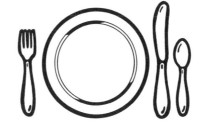

30

MUSIC _____

31

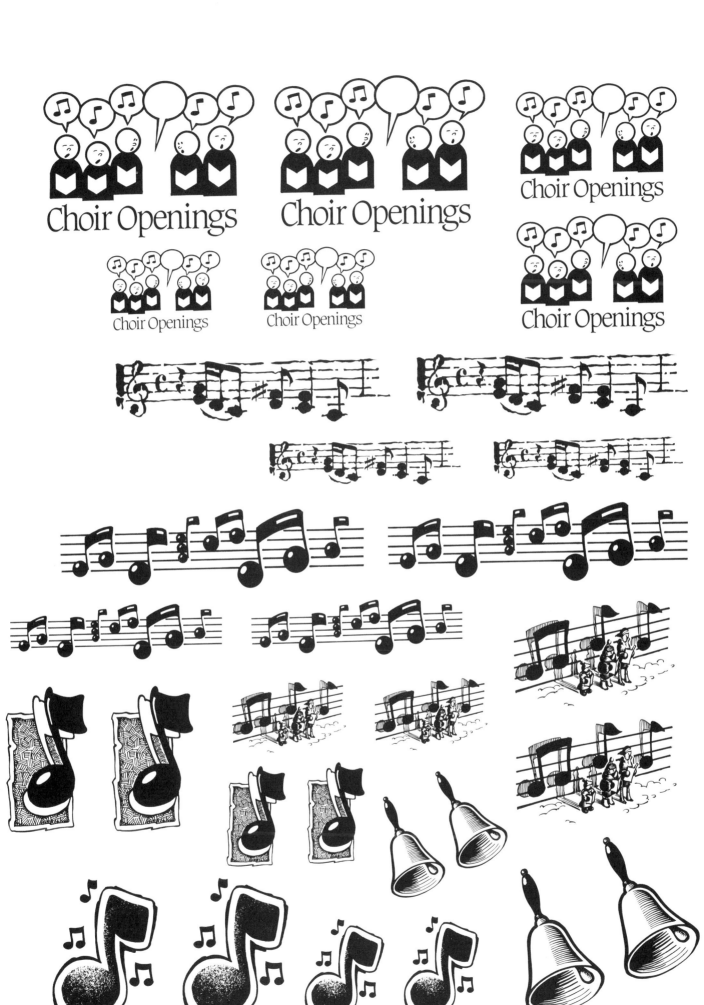

PEOPLE _____

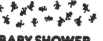

CHILDREN

BABY SHOWER   **BABY SHOWER**

BABY SHOWER   **BABY SHOWER**

Children's Church

Children's Ministry

DAYCARE

34

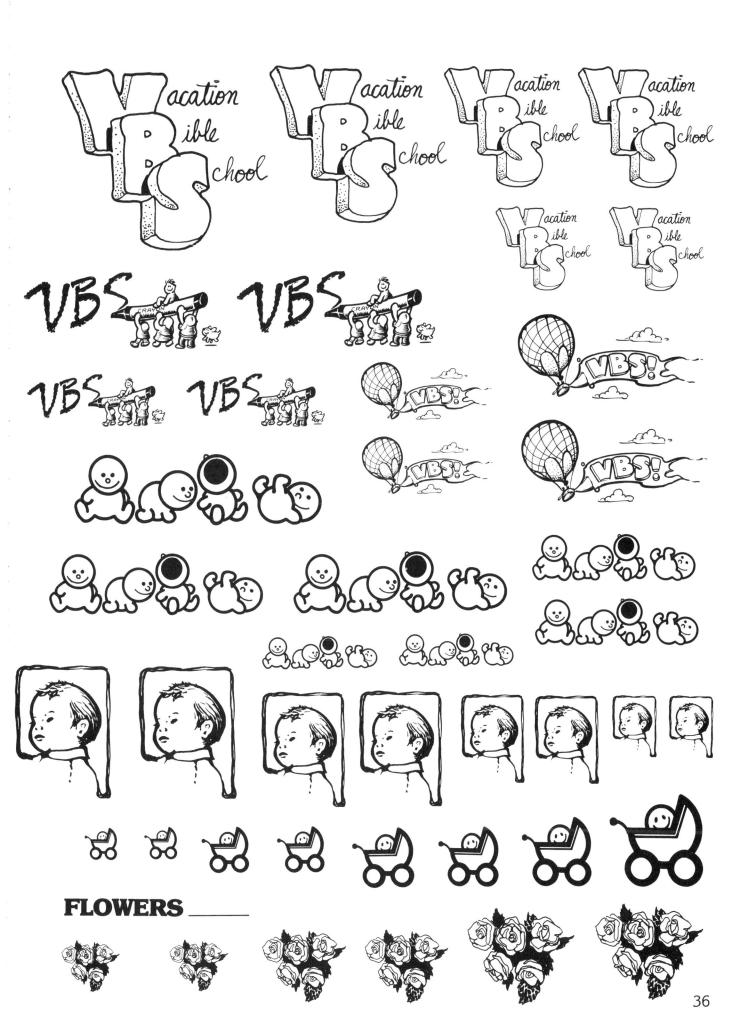

FLOWERS _____

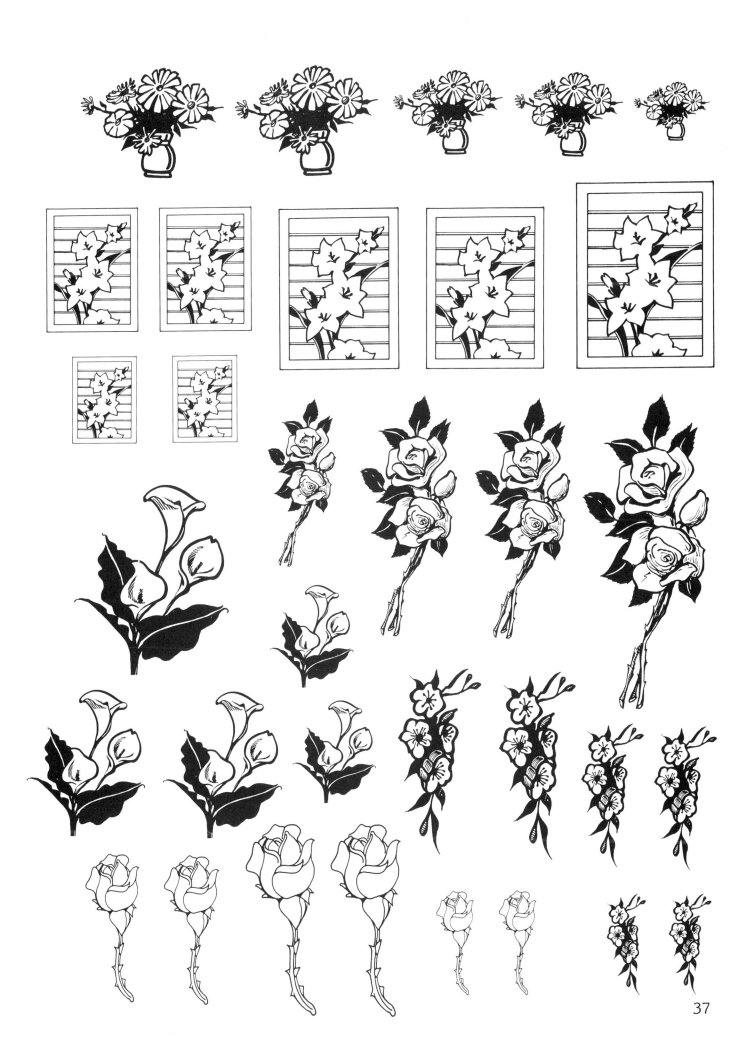

37

ANIMALS _____

DATES AND SEASONS

 AUGUST  AUGUST  AUGUST

 AUGUST

 SEPT.  SEPT.  SEPT.

 SEPT.  SEPT.  SEPT.  SEPT.

 OCT.  OCT.  OCT.  OCT.

 NOV. NOV.  NOV. NOV.

 DEC.  DEC.  DEC.  DEC.

 DEC. DEC.

 Spring Spring Spring Summer

 Summer Summer Summer

 FALL  FALL  FALL  FALL

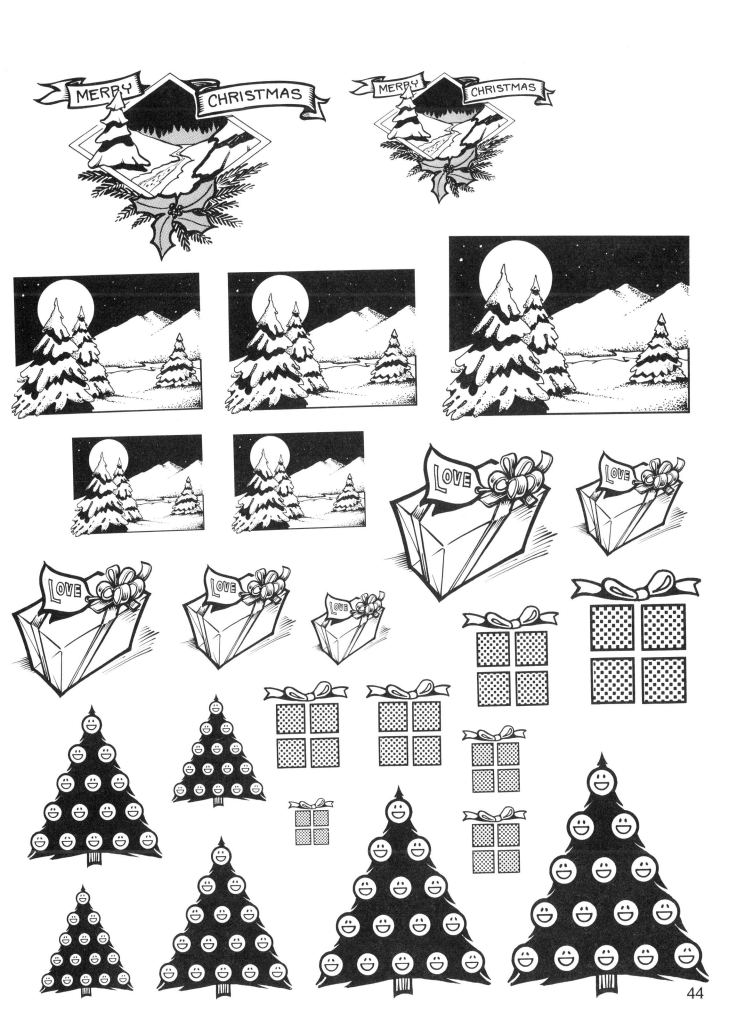

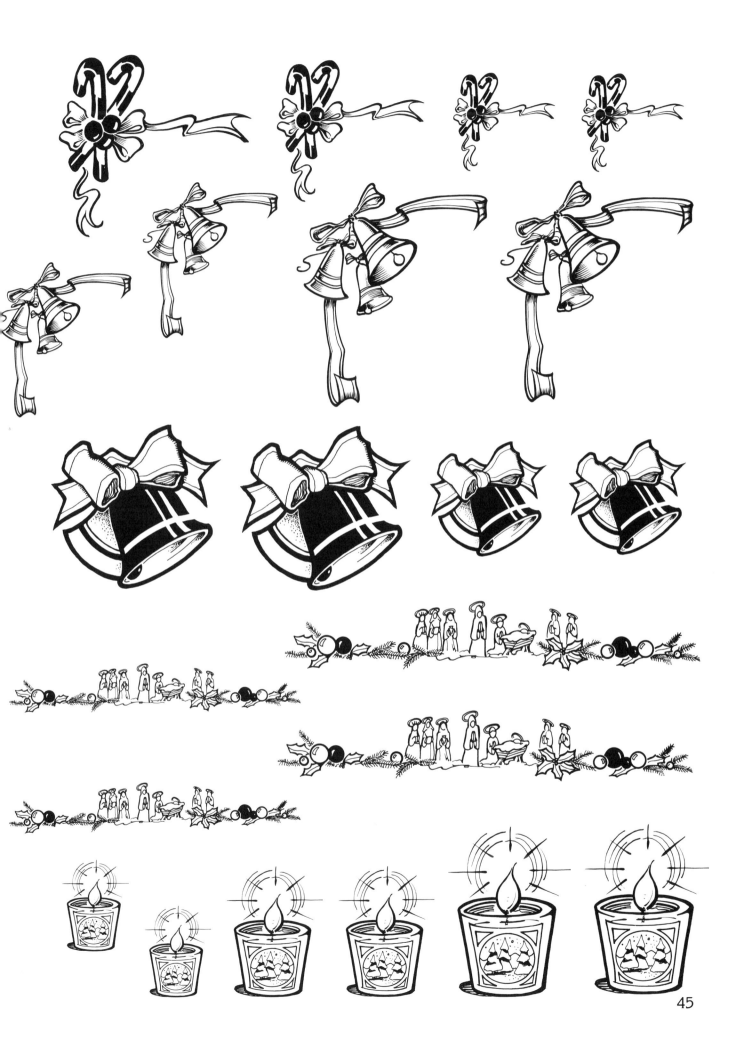

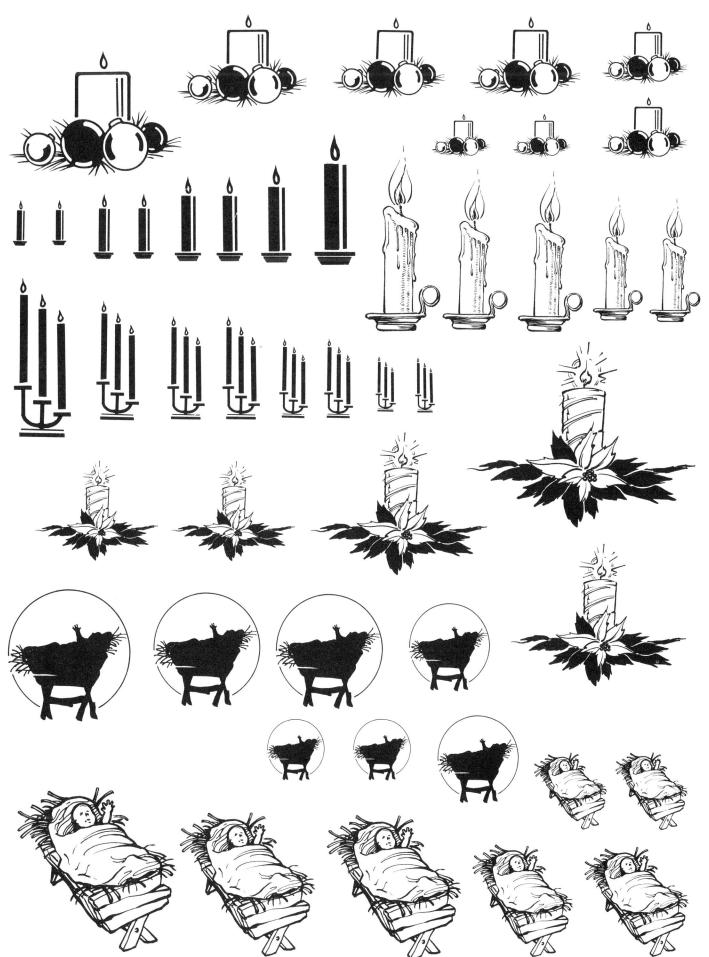

TRANSPORTATION

MAPS

47

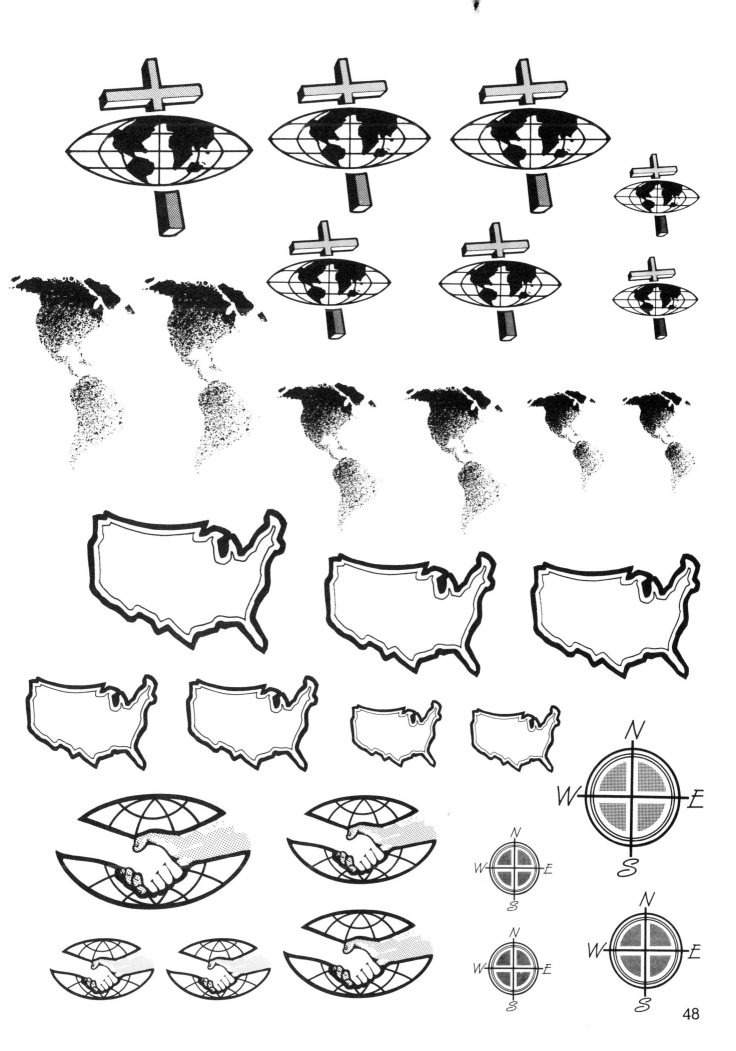

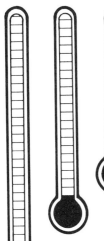
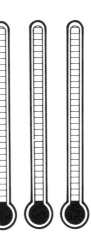

Handicapped News

Handicapped News

Handicapped News

Handicapped News

Handicapped News

Handicapped News

Handicapped News

Handicapped News

In the Hospital

In the Hospital

In the Hospital

In the Hospital

In the Hospital

In the Hospital

In the Hospital

In the Hospital

51

53

S.O.S! S.O.S! S.O.S! S.O.S!

Sponsors Needed

Sponsors Needed

Sponsors Needed

Sponsors Needed

TAPES

TAPES

TAPES

TAPES

TAPES

Visit our TAPE LIBRARY

Visit our TAPE LIBRARY

Visit our TAPE LIBRARY

thank You!

thank You!

thank You!

thank You!

TIME CHANGE

TIME CHANGE

TIME CHANGE

TIME CHANGE

TIME CHANGE

TIME CHANGE

55

ASSORTED "ALERTS" AND MISCELLANEOUS ART

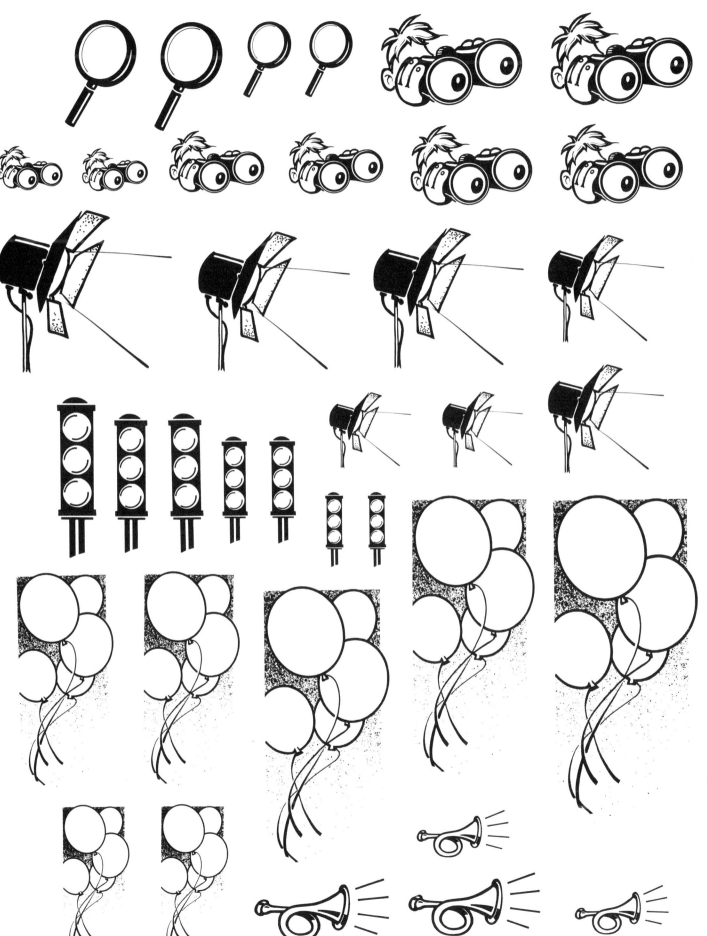

57

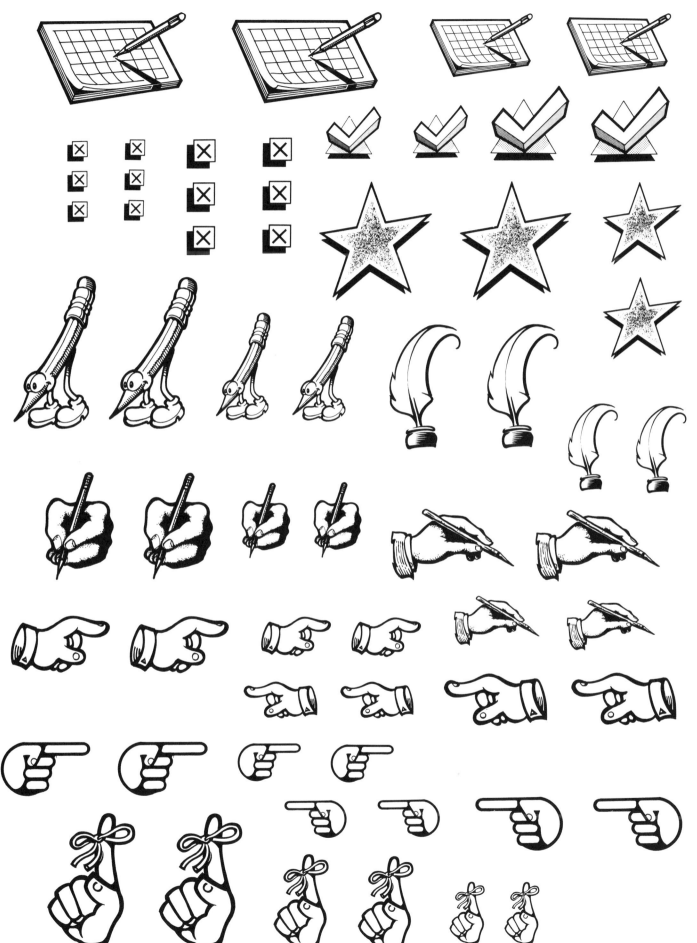

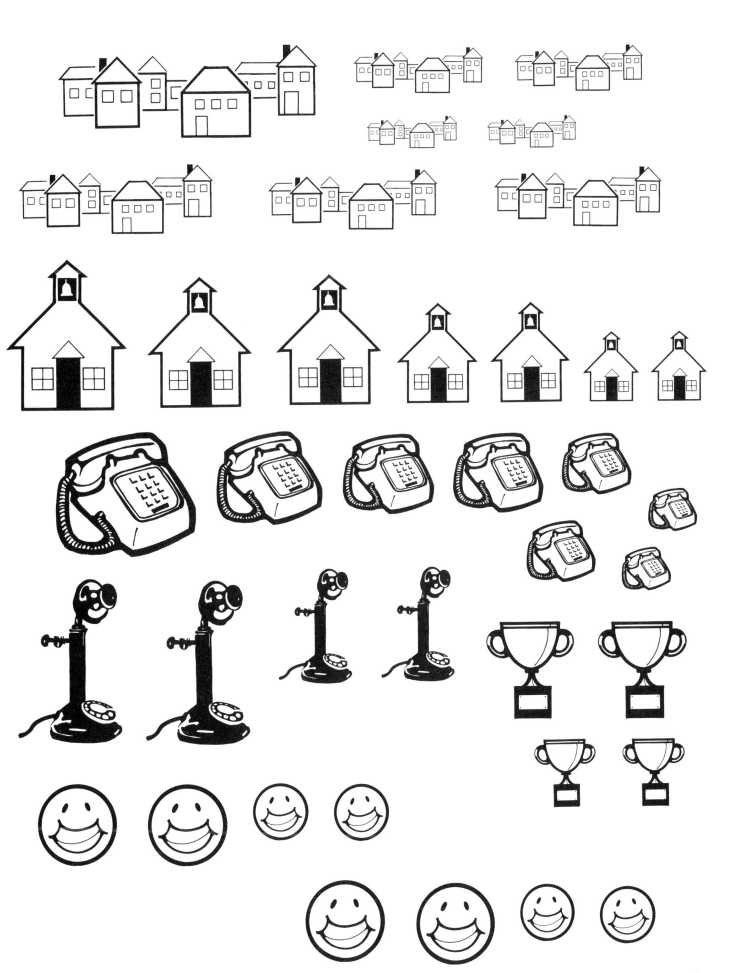

BORDERS, BANNERS AND DESIGNS

Use these to add emphasis to your bulletin's most important notes and messages.

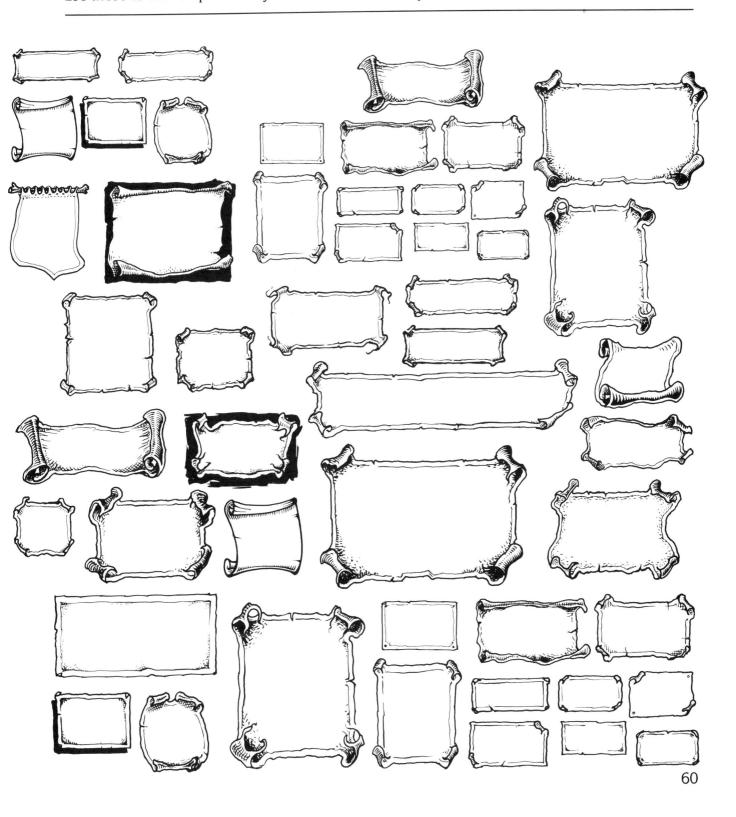

60

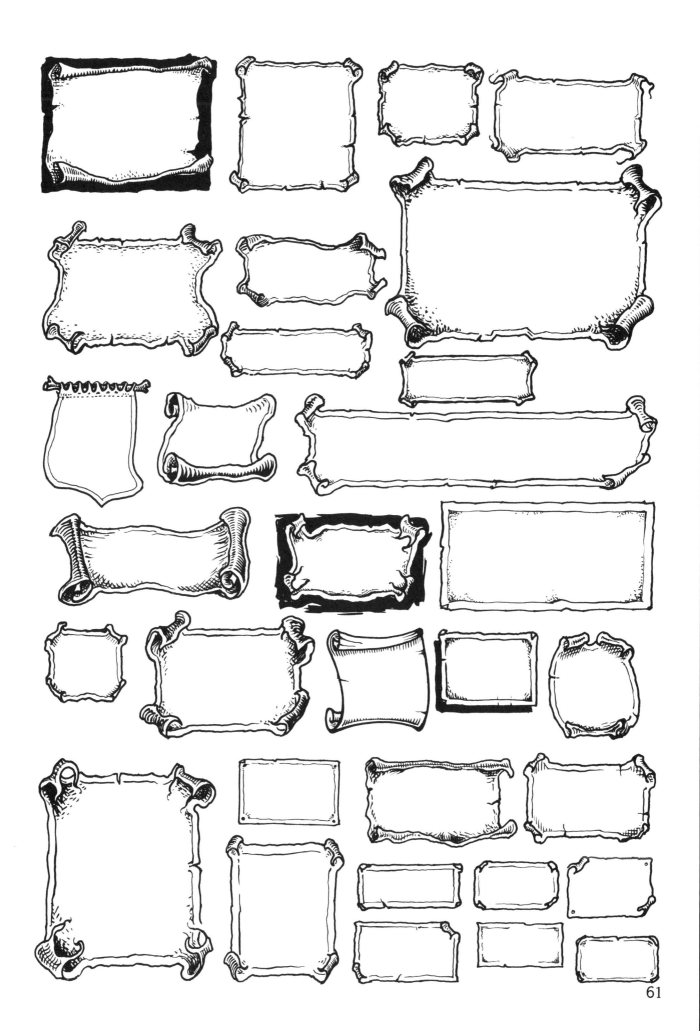

61

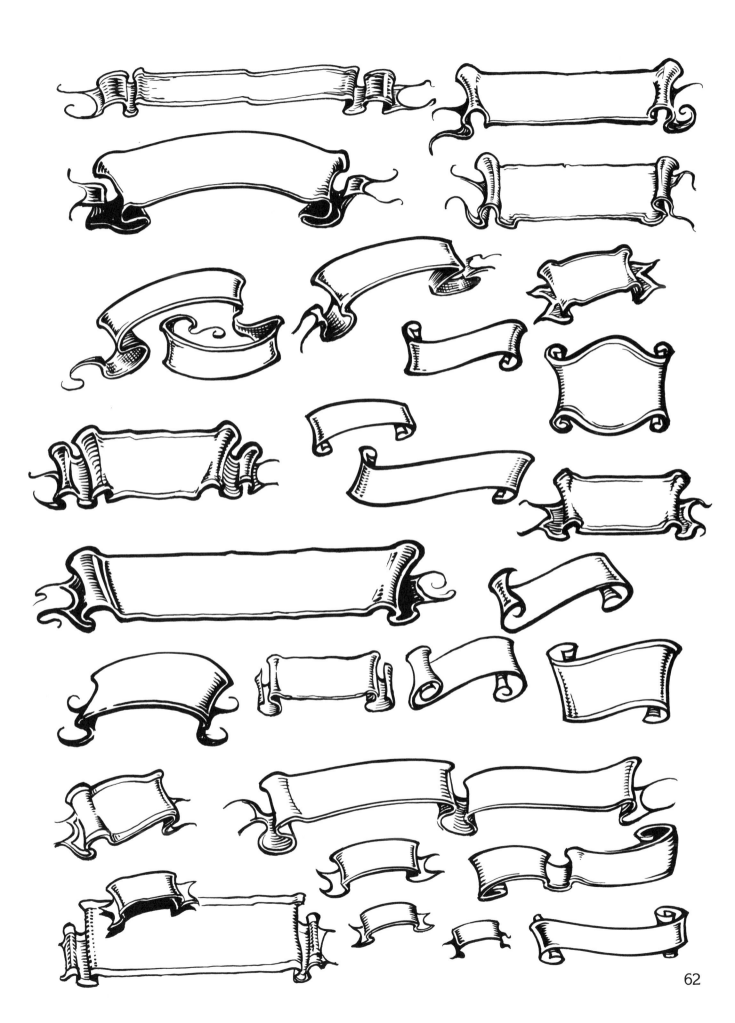

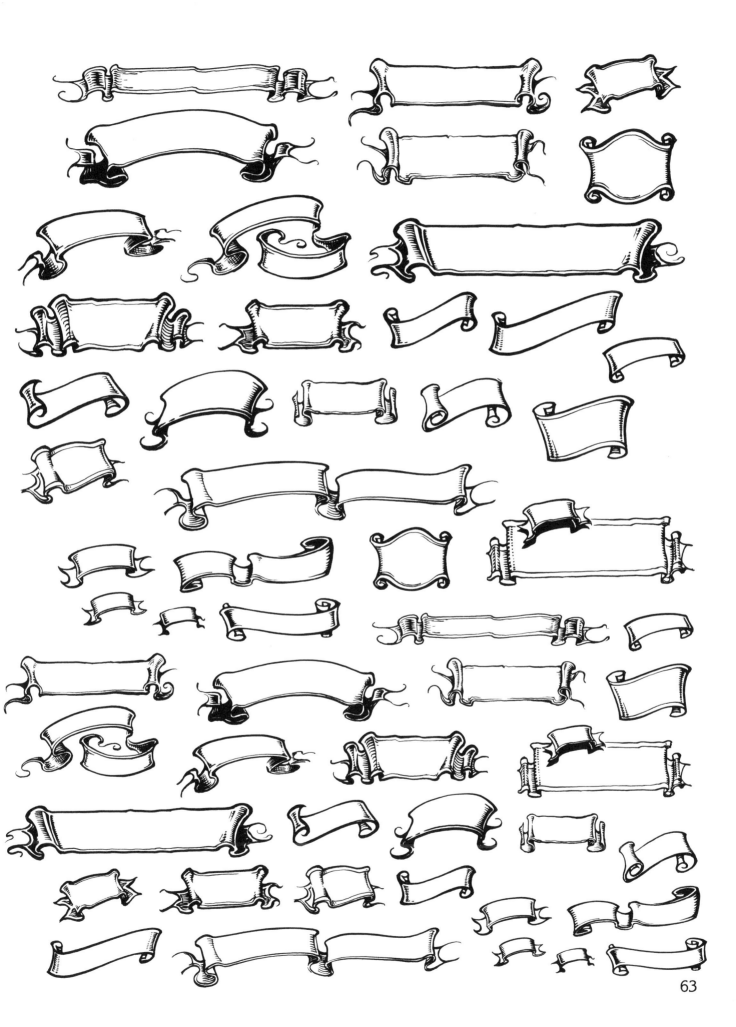

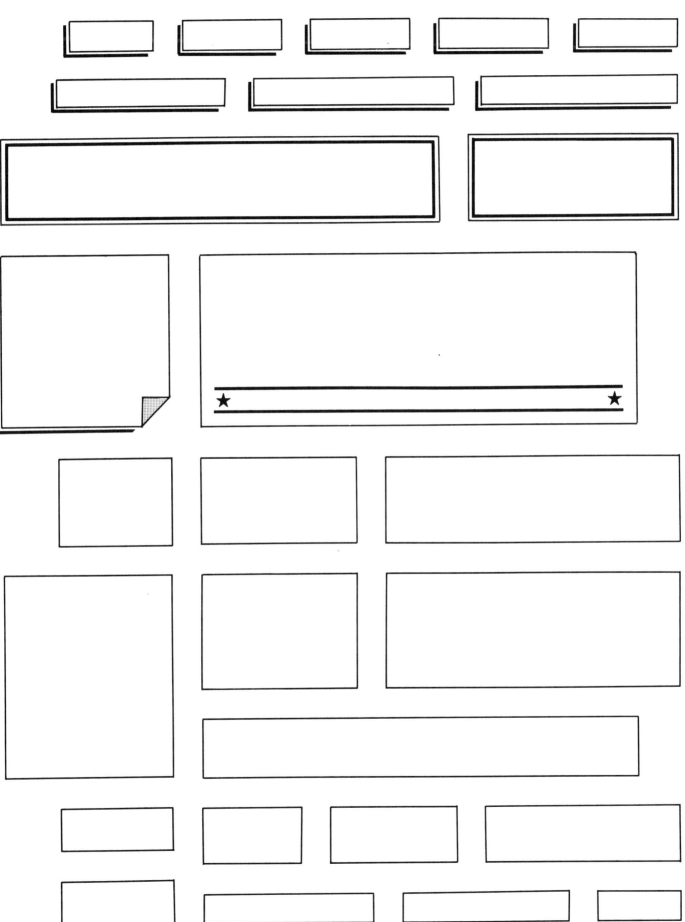

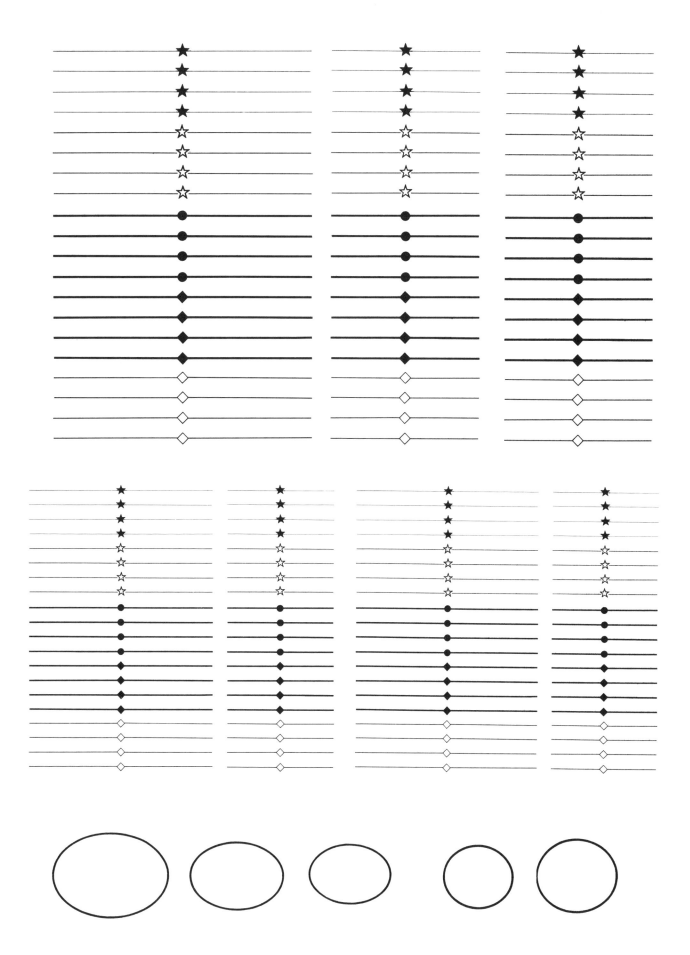

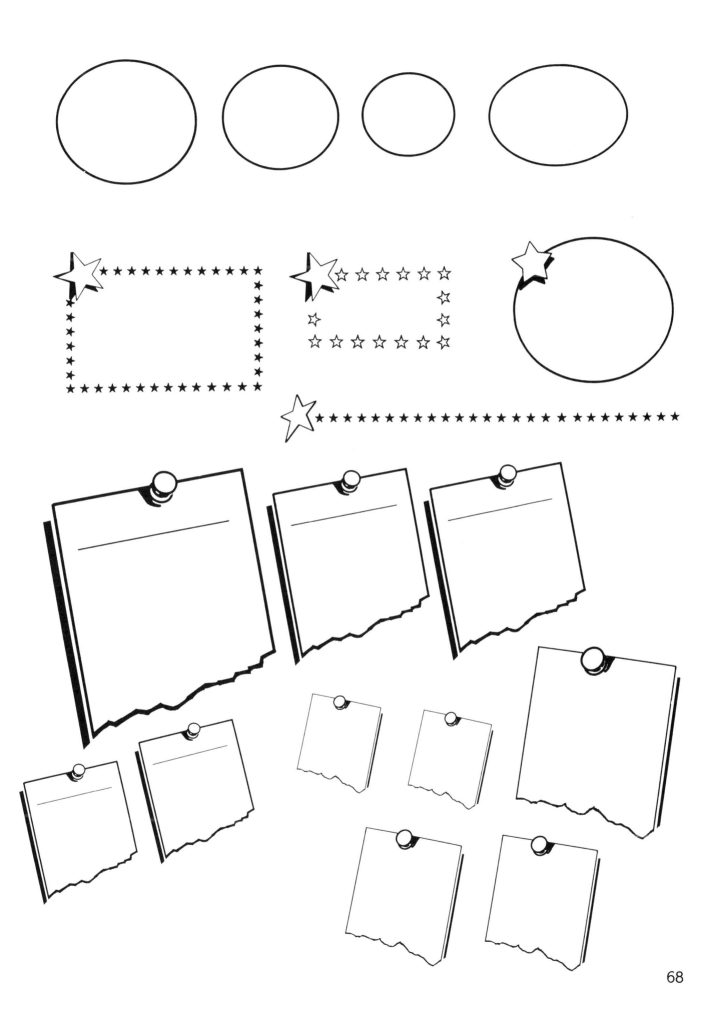

HEADERS AND LOGOS

Well over 500 commonly needed titles and phrases have been typeset to save you time and expense, and to provide you still another way to make your bulletins look professionally produced. Each has been typeset in two styles. Additionally, about 150 phrases (beginning on this page) have been hand designed for even greater visual appeal.

A valuable suggestion: You can create a nearly limitless variety of headlines and mastheads by cutting and combining two or more of ours. For example, "Staff Meeting" and "Church Picnic" can be combined to form "Church Staff Picnic." Also, you can render a plural word singular by snipping off the ending.

ADVANCEMENT SUNDAY   ADVANCEMENT SUNDAY   ADVANCEMENT SUNDAY

ADVANCEMENT SUNDAY   ADVANCEMENT SUNDAY   ADVANCEMENT SUNDAY   ADVANCEMENT SUNDAY

ADVANCEMENT SUNDAY

Advent   Advent   Advent   Advent   Advent

Advent   Advent   Advent

AGAPE LOVE   AGAPE LOVE   AGAPE LOVE

AGAPE LOVE   AGAPE LOVE   AGAPE LOVE   AGAPE LOVE   AGAPE LOVE

ALSO... ALSO... ALSO... ALSO... ALSO...

ALSO...

ALSO... ALSO...

AMBASSADORS   AMBASSADORS   AMBASSADORS

AMBASSADORS   AMBASSADORS   AMBASSADORS

AMBASSADORS   AMBASSADORS

AND...

AND... AND... AND... AND... AND... AND... AND...

69

Announcement Announcement Announcement

Announcement Announcement Announcement

Announcement Announcement Attendance Attendance

Attendance Attendance Attendance Attendance

Attendance Attendance

•Attention, **Men:** •Attention, **Men:** •Attention, **Men:**

•Attention, **Men:** •Attention, **Men:** •Attention, **Men:**

Attention, Women •Attention, **Men:** •Attention, **Men:**

Attention, Women Attention, Women Attention, Women

Attention, Women Attention, Women Attention, Women Attention, Women

AWARDS BANQUET AWARDS BANQUET AWARDS BANQUET

AWARDS BANQUET AWARDS BANQUET AWARDS BANQUET

AWARDS BANQUET

✳Babies ✳Babies ✳Babies ✳Babies

✳Babies ✳Babies ✳Babies ✳Babies

BACK TO School BACK TO School

BACK TO School BACK TO School BACK TO School

BACK TO School BACK TO School

BACK TO School BACK TO School BACK TO School

Backyard
Bible Study

Backyard
Bible Study

Backyard
Bible Study

Backyard
Bible Study

Backyard
Bible Study

Backyard
Bible Study

Backyard
Bible Study

Banquet

Banquet

Banquet

Banquet

Banquet

Banquet

Banquet

BIRTHS

BIRTHS

BIRTHS

BIRTHS

BIRTHS

BIRTHS

BIRTHS

BOOKS
Needed

BOOKS
Needed

BOOKS
Needed

BOOKS
Needed

BOOKS
Needed

BOOKS
Needed

BOOKS
Needed

Breakfast

Breakfast

Breakfast

Breakfast

Breakfast

Breakfast

·BUDGET·

·BUDGET·

·BUDGET·

·BUDGET·

·BUDGET·

·BUDGET·

·BUDGET·

·BUDGET·

•Budget MEETING   •Budget MEETING   •Budget MEETING   •Budget MEETING

•Budget MEETING   •Budget MEETING   •Budget MEETING

•Budget MEETING

-BUS- -BUS- -BUS-

-BUS- -BUS- -BUS- -BUS- -BUS-

CALENDAR of events   CALENDAR of events   CALENDAR of events   CALENDAR of events

CALENDAR of events   CALENDAR of events   CALENDAR of events   CALENDAR of events

CAMP! CAMP! CAMP! CAMP!
CAMP!

CAMP! CAMP! CAMP!

Career WOMEN   Career WOMEN   Career WOMEN   Career WOMEN

Career WOMEN   Career WOMEN   Career WOMEN

Career WOMEN   Celebration   Celebration

Celebration   Celebration   Celebration   Celebration

Celebration   CHOIR   CHOIR   CHOIR

Celebration   CHOIR   CHOIR

CHOIR   CHOIR   CHOIR

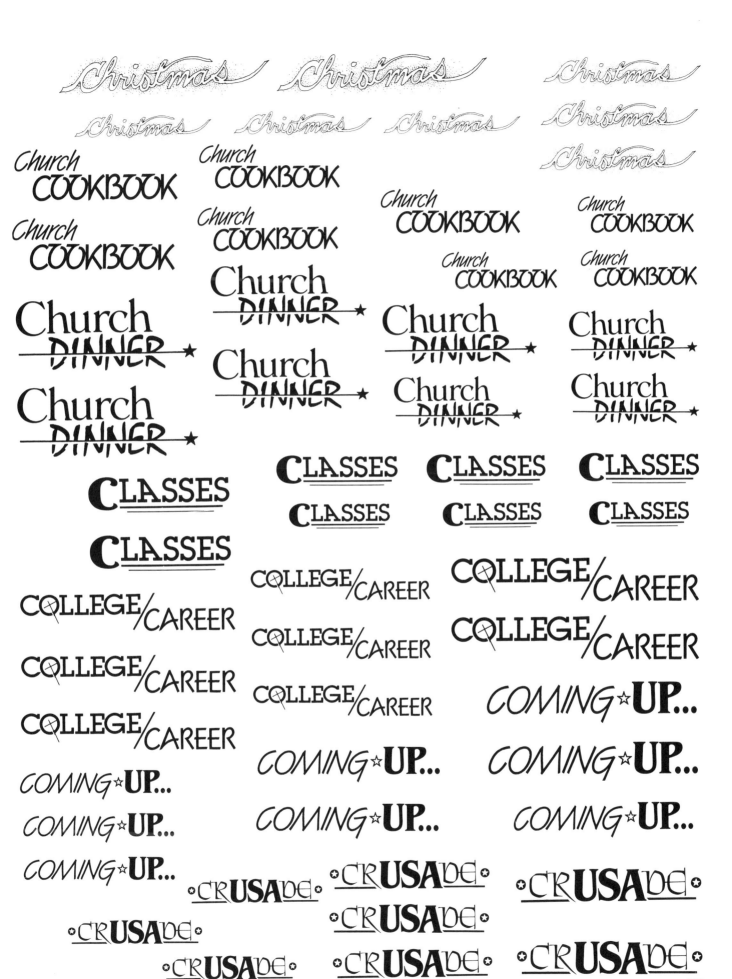

Christmas Christmas Christmas
Christmas Christmas Christmas Christmas
Christmas

Church COOKBOOK
Church COOKBOOK
Church COOKBOOK
Church COOKBOOK
Church COOKBOOK
Church COOKBOOK
Church COOKBOOK
Church COOKBOOK

Church DINNER ★
Church DINNER ★
Church DINNER ★
Church DINNER ★
Church DINNER ★
Church DINNER ★
Church DINNER ★

CLASSES
CLASSES
CLASSES
CLASSES
CLASSES
CLASSES
CLASSES

COLLEGE/CAREER
COLLEGE/CAREER
COLLEGE/CAREER
COLLEGE/CAREER
COLLEGE/CAREER
COLLEGE/CAREER
COLLEGE/CAREER

COMING ★ UP...
COMING ★ UP...
COMING ★ UP...
COMING ★ UP...
COMING ★ UP...
COMING ★ UP...
COMING ★ UP...

CRUSADE
CRUSADE
CRUSADE
CRUSADE
CRUSADE
CRUSADE
CRUSADE

DATE **DATE** **DATE** **DATE** **DATE**

DATE **DATE** **DATE**

DAY CAMP DAY CAMP

DAY CAMP DAY CAMP DAY CAMP DAY CAMP

DAYSCHOOL *DAYSCHOOL* **DAY CAMP** **DAY CAMP**

DAYSCHOOL *DAYSCHOOL* *DAYSCHOOL* *DAYSCHOOL*

DAYSCHOOL *DAYSCHOOL* **D**eacons **D**eacons

Deacons **D**eacons **D**eacons **D**eacons **D**eacons **D**eacons

DEADLINE **DEAD**LINE **DEAD**LINE **DEAD**LINE

DEADLINE **DEAD**LINE **DEAD**LINE **DEAD**LINE

DEATH DEATH DEATH DEATH DEATH

DEATH DEATH DEATH

Dedication Service *Dedication Service* *Dedication Service* *Dedication Service* *Dedication Service*

Dedication Service *Dedication Service* *Dedication Service* *Dinner* *Dinner*

Dinner *Dinner* *Dinner*

Dinner *Dinner* *Dinner*

DIRECTORY *Photos* **DIRECTORY** *Photos* **DIRECTORY** *Photos* **DIRECTORY** *Photos*

DIRECTORY *Photos* **DIRECTORY** *Photos* **DIRECTORY** *Photos* **DIRECTORY** *Photos*

74

DIVORCE RECOVERY WORKSHOP

DIVORCE RECOVERY WORKSHOP

DIVORCE RECOVERY WORKSHOP

DIVORCE RECOVERY WORKSHOP

DIVORCE RECOVERY WORKSHOP

DIVORCE RECOVERY WORKSHOP

DIVORCE RECOVERY WORKSHOP

DIVORCE RECOVERY WORKSHOP

DONATION DONATION DONATION

DONATION DONATION DONATION

DONATION DONATION

DON'T FORGET: DON'T FORGET: DON'T FORGET: DON'T FORGET: DON'T FORGET:

DON'T FORGET: DON'T FORGET:

Easter Easter Easter Easter Easter

DON'T FORGET:

Easter Easter Easter

EASTER EASTER

EASTER EASTER EASTER

EASTER

Easter Easter Easter Easter

Easter Easter Easter Easter

ELDERS ELDERS ELDERS ELDERS ELDERS ELDERS

New ELDERS New ELDERS New ELDERS New ELDERS ELDERS

ELDERS

New ELDERS New ELDERS New ELDERS New ELDERS

ELECTIVES *ELECTIVES* *ELECTIVES*

ELECTIVES *ELECTIVES* *ELECTIVES*

ELECTIVES *ELECTIVES*

ENROLL *NOW!* **ENROLL** *NOW!* **ENROLL** *NOW!* **ENROLL** *NOW!*

ENROLL *NOW!* **ENROLL** *NOW!* **ENROLL** *NOW!* **ENROLL** *NOW!*

Engaged: Engaged: Engaged: Engaged:

FALL

Engaged: Engaged: Engaged: Engaged:

FALL **FALL** **FALL** **FALL** **FALL** **FALL** **FALL**

FAMILY .....FUN... *FAMILY* .....FUN... *FAMILY* .....FUN... *FAMILY* .....FUN...

FAMILY .....FUN... *FAMILY* .....FUN... *FAMILY* .....FUN... *FAMILY* .....FUN...

FAMILY *News* FAMILY *News* FAMILY *News* FAMILY *News* FAMILY *News*

FAMILY *News* FAMILY *News* FAMILY *News*

Famine *Relief* Famine *Relief*

Famine *Relief* Famine *Relief* Famine *Relief* Famine *Relief*

Famine *Relief* Famine *Relief*

Famine *Relief*

Farewell... *Farewell...* *Farewell...*

Farewell... *Farewell...*

Farewell... *Farewell...* *Farewell...*

FREE **FREE** **FREE** **FREE** **FREE**

FREE **FREE** **FREE**

GIVE BLOOD *GIVE* BLOOD *GIVE* BLOOD *GIVE* BLOOD

GIVE BLOOD *GIVE* BLOOD *GIVE* BLOOD *GIVE* BLOOD

Give Life Give Life Give Life Give Life Give Life

Good Friday Good Friday Good Friday Give Life Give Life Give Life

Good Friday Good Friday Good Friday Good Friday Good Friday

GOOD NEWS GOOD NEWS GOOD NEWS GOOD NEWS

GOOD NEWS GOOD NEWS GOOD NEWS

GOOD NEWS Graduation

Graduation Graduation

Graduation

Graduation Graduation

Graduation Graduation

Guest Speaker

Guest Speaker Guest Speaker Guest Speaker Guest Speaker

Guest Speaker Guest Speaker Guest Speaker

77

HAVE YOU Heard?   HAVE YOU Heard?   HAVE YOU Heard?   HAVE YOU Heard?

HAVE YOU Heard?   HAVE YOU Heard?   HAVE YOU Heard?   HAVE YOU Heard?

HELP!   HELP!   HELP!

HELP!   HELP!   HELP!   HELP!   HELP!

HELP NEEDED   HELP NEEDED   HELP NEEDED

HELP NEEDED   HELP NEEDED   HELP NEEDED   HELP NEEDED

HELPING HANDS   HELPING HANDS   HELPING HANDS   HELPING HANDS   HELP NEEDED

HELPING HANDS   HELPING HANDS   HELPING HANDS   HELPING HANDS   Hey, Kids!

Hey, Kids!

Hey, Kids!

Hey, Kids!   Hey, Kids!

Hey, Kids!   Hey, Kids!   Hey, Kids!

In Memory Of...

In Memory Of...   In Memory Of...   In Memory Of...   In Memory Of...

In Memory Of...   In Memory Of...   In Memory Of...   Invitation

Invitation   Invitation   Invitation   Invitation   Invitation

Invitation   Invitation   It's not TOO LATE   It's not TOO LATE

It's not TOO LATE   It's not TOO LATE   It's not TOO LATE

It's not TOO LATE   It's not TOO LATE   It's not TOO LATE

Join Us! *Join Us!* *Join Us!* *Join Us!*
Join Us! *Join Us!* *Join Us!* *Join Us!*

KICK OFF! KICK OFF! KICK OFF! KICK OFF! KICK OFF!
KICK OFF! KICK OFF! KICK OFF! Koinonia Koinonia
Koinonia Koinonia Koinonia Koinonia Koinonia Koinonia

Labor of LOVE   Labor of LOVE   Labor of LOVE   Labor of LOVE

Labor of LOVE   Labor of LOVE   Labor of LOVE   Labor of LOVE

Last Supper   Last Supper   Last Supper   Last Supper   Last Supper
Last Supper   Last Supper   Last Supper

•Lay Ministers•
•Lay Ministers•   •Lay Ministers•   •Lay Ministers•
•Lay Ministers•   •Lay Ministers•   •Lay Ministers•   •Lay Ministers•

LENT LENT LENT LENT LENT LENT LENT LENT

LIBRARY   LIBRARY   LIBRARY   LIBRARY
LIBRARY   LIBRARY   LIBRARY   LIBRARY

LITERATURE
—*TABLE*—
LITERATURE
—*TABLE*—
LITERATURE
—*TABLE*—
LITERATURE
—*TABLE*—

LITERATURE
—*TABLE*—
LITERATURE
—*TABLE*—
LITERATURE
—*TABLE*—
LITERATURE
—*TABLE*—

THE**LOGOS** THE**LOGOS** THE**LOGOS** The Lord's Business

THE**LOGOS** THE**LOGOS** THE**LOGOS** The Lord's Business

THE**LOGOS** THE**LOGOS**

Lost: Lost: Lost: The Lord's Business The Lord's Business The Lord's Business

Lost: Lost: Lost: The Lord's Business The Lord's Business The Lord's Business

Lost: Lost: **LOST**&*FOUND* **LOST**&*FOUND*

LOST&*FOUND* **LOST**&*FOUND* **LOST**&*FOUND*

LOST&*FOUND* **LOST**&*FOUND* *MAIL* *MAIL*

MAIL *MAIL* *MAIL* *MAIL* *MAIL* Make *Plans*

MAIL

Make *Plans* Make *Plans* Make *Plans* Make *Plans* Make *Plans* Make *Plans*

Make *Plans* MEDIA MEDIA MEDIA C·E·N·T·E·R

C·E·N·T·E·R C·E·N·T·E·R MEDIA C·E·N·T·E·R

MEDIA MEDIA MEDIA MEDIA
C·E·N·T·E·R C·E·N·T·E·R C·E·N·T·E·R C·E·N·T·E·R

Membership Classes Membership Classes Membership Classes Membership Classes

Membership Classes Membership Classes Membership Classes Membership Classes

MEMO: MEMO: MEMO:

MEMO: MEMO: MEMO: MEMO: MEMO:

Miracles! Miracles! Miracles! Miracles! Miracles! Miracles!

Our Mission: Our Mission: Our Mission: Miracles! Miracles!

Our Mission: Our Mission: Our Mission: Our Mission:

Our Mission:

MissionS MissionS MissionS MissionS

MissionS MissionS MissionS MissionS

MOVIE Night MOVIE Night MOVIE Night MOVIE Night MOVIE Night

MOVIE Night MOVIE Night MOVIE Night

NEW! NEW! NEW! NEW! NEW!

NEW! NEW! NEW!

BIG NEWS: BIG NEWS: BIG NEWS: BIG NEWS:

BIG NEWS: BIG NEWS: BIG NEWS: BIG NEWS:

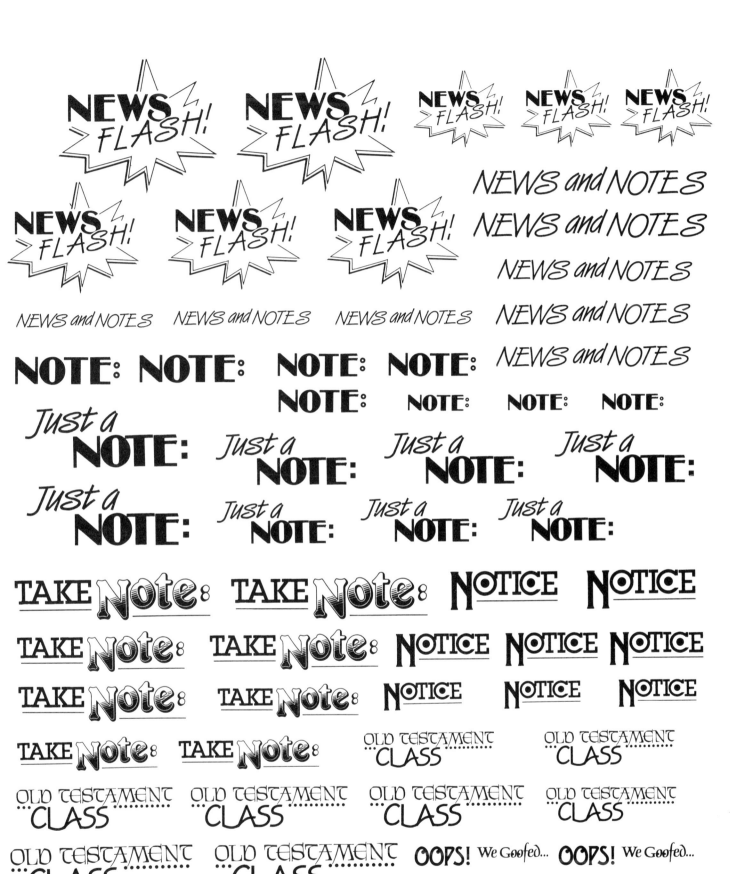

OPPORTUNITIES *OPPORTUNITIES* *OPPORTUNITIES*

OPPORTUNITIES *OPPORTUNITIES* *OPPORTUNITIES*

OPPORTUNITIES *OPPORTUNITIES*

OUR *Vision*   OUR *Vision*   OUR *Vision*   OUR *Vision*   OUR *Vision*   OUR *Vision*

OUTLOOK   **OUTLOOK**   OUR *Vision*   OUR *Vision*

OUTLOOK   **OUTLOOK**   **OUTLOOK**   *Passover*

OUTLOOK   **OUTLOOK**   **OUTLOOK**

Passover   *Passover*   *Passover*   *Passover*   *Passover*   *Passover*

Passover   *From the* **PASTOR**—   *From the* **PASTOR**—

From the **PASTOR**—   *From the* **PASTOR**—   *From the* **PASTOR**—

From the **PASTOR**—   *From the* **PASTOR**—   *From the* **PASTOR**—

Pastor's NOTES   Pastor's NOTES   Pastor's NOTES

Pastor's NOTES   Pastor's NOTES   Pastor's NOTES

Pastor's NOTES   Pastor's NOTES

All-Church ★*PICNIC*★

All-Church ★*PICNIC*★   All-Church ★*PICNIC*★   All-Church ★*PICNIC*★   All-Church ★*PICNIC*★

All-Church ★*PICNIC*★   All-Church ★*PICNIC*★   All-Church ★*PICNIC*★

·Picnic· ·Picnic· ·Picnic·

·Picnic· ·Picnic· ·Picnic·

·Picnic· ·Picnic·

PIONEER GIRLS   PIONEER GIRLS   PIONEER GIRLS   PIONEER GIRLS

PIONEER GIRLS   PIONEER GIRLS   PIONEER GIRLS   PIONEER GIRLS

★PLEASE★ ★PLEASE★ ★PLEASE★ ★PLEASE★ ★PLEASE★ ★PLEASE★

★PLEASE★ ★PLEASE★   PLEASE PRAY   PLEASE PRAY   PLEASE PRAY   PLEASE PRAY

Thank you for Praying   PLEASE PRAY   PLEASE PRAY   PLEASE PRAY   PLEASE PRAY

Thank you for Praying   Thank you for Praying   Thank you for Praying   Thank you for Praying

Thank you for Praying   Thank you for Praying   Thank you for Praying   ★PRAISE!★

★PRAISE!★   ★PRAISE!★   ★PRAISE!★   ★PRAISE!★

    ★PRAISE!★   ★PRAISE!★

PREVIEW: PREVIEW:

PREVIEW: PREVIEW: ★PRAISE!★

PREVIEW: PREVIEW: PREVIEW: PREVIEW:

PSSST! PSSST! PSSST! PSSST!

PSSST! PSSST! PSSST! PSSST!

RALLy

RALLy RALLy RALLy REJOICE!

RALLy RALLy RALLy RALLy REJOICE!

REJOICE! REJOICE! REJOICE! REJOICE!

REJOICE! REJOICE!

REMINDER: REMINDER:

REMINDER: REMINDER:

REMINDER: REMINDER:

REMINDER: REMINDER:

Fall RETREAT Fall RETREAT Fall RETREAT

Fall RETREAT Fall RETREAT Fall RETREAT

Fall RETREAT Fall RETREAT

SabbatH SabbatH

SabbatH SabbatH

SabbatH

Seminar SabbatH SabbatH SabbatH

Seminar Seminar Seminar Seminar

SENIOR SENIOR Seminar Seminar
Saints Saints

SENIOR SENIOR SENIOR SENIOR
Saints Saints Saints Saints

Share Your Faith! Share Your Faith! Share Your Faith! Share Your Faith!

Share Your Faith! Share Your Faith! Share Your Faith! Share Your Faith!

Schedule: *Schedule:*   *Schedule:*   *Schedule:*

Schedule: *Schedule:*   *Schedule:*   *Schedule:*   *Schedule:*

SIGN UP   SIGN UP   SIGN UP   SIGN UP

SIGN UP   SIGN UP   SIGN UP   SIGN UP

SPECIAL events   SPECIAL events   SPECIAL events   SPECIAL events

SPECIAL events   SPECIAL events   SPECIAL events

SPECIAL events   SPECIAL NEED: SPECIAL NEED: SPECIAL NEED:

SPECIAL NEED: SPECIAL NEED: SPECIAL NEED: SPECIAL NEED: SPECIAL NEED:

Special Offering   Special Offering

Special Offering   Special Offering   SPRING

Special Offering   Special Offering   SPRING

Special Offering   Special Offering

SPRING   SPRING   SPRING   SPRING   SPRING

SPRING

SPRING FLING   SPRING FLING

SPRING FLING

SPRING FLING   SPRING FLING

SPRING FLING   SPRING FLING

SUMMER SUMMER SUMMER SUMMER
SUMMER SUMMER

SUMMER SUMMER SUMMER

Thanksgiving *Thanksgiving* *Thanksgiving*

Thanksgiving *Thanksgiving* *Thanksgiving*

Thanksgiving

Thank You! Thank You! Thank You! Thank You! Thank You! Thank You!

Thank You!

NOTE OF *Thanks...* NOTE OF *Thanks...* NOTE OF *Thanks...* NOTE OF *Thanks...*

Thank You!

NOTE OF *Thanks...* NOTE OF *Thanks...* NOTE OF *Thanks...* NOTE OF *Thanks...*

THOT:

THOT: THOT: THOT: THOT: THOT:

THOT: THOT:

TV *Worth Watching* **TV** *Worth Watching*

TV *Worth Watching* **TV** *Worth Watching* **TV** *Worth Watching* **TV** *Worth Watching*

TV *Worth Watching* **TV** *Worth Watching*

UPDATE UPDATE UPDATE

UPDATE UPDATE UPDATE UPDATE UPDATE

VBS **VBS**

VBS *RALLY* **VBS** *RALLY*

VBS *RALLY* **VBS** **VBS**

VBS *RALLY*

VBS *RALLY* **VBS** *RALLY* **VBS** *RALLY*

VBS **VBS**

Walk-a-thon   Walk-a-thon   Walk-a-thon   Walk-a-thon

Walk-a-thon   Walk-a-thon   Walk-a-thon   Walk-a-thon

ThisWEEK   ThisWEEK   ThisWEEK   ThisWEEK

ThisWEEK   ThisWEEK   ThisWEEK   ThisWEEK

◆WELCOME!◆   ◆WELCOME!◆   ◆WELCOME!◆

◆WELCOME!◆   ◆WELCOME!◆

◆WELCOME!◆

◆WELCOME!◆   ◆WELCOME!◆

Welcome
HOME!

Welcome
HOME!

Welcome
HOME!

Welcome
HOME!

Welcome
HOME!

Welcome
HOME!

Welcome
HOME!

Welcome
HOME!

We need YOU....

We need YOU....

We need YOU....

We need YOU....

We need YOU....

We need YOU....

We need YOU....

We need YOU....

Winter   Winter   Winter   Winter

Winter   Winter   Winter   Winter

WORSHIP   WORSHIP   WORSHIP   WORSHIP

WORSHIP   WORSHIP

WORSHIP   WORSHIP

YES!✓   YES!✓   YES!✓

YES!✓   YES!✓   YES!✓   YES!✓   YES!✓

Adult Fellowship
Advancement Sunday
Advent
Aerobics
Afterglow
Agape Love
All Are Welcome
All-Church Picnic
Also . . .
Ambassadors
And . . .
And the Lord Added
  to His Church
Announcements
Anniversaries
At Home and Abroad
Attendance
Attention, Men
Attention, Parents
Attention, Women
Awards Banquet

Babies
Baby Shower
Back to School
Backyard Bible Study
Bake Sale
Banquet
Baptism Service
Barbecue
Baseball
Basketball
Benevolence Fund
Bereans
Bible School
Bible Study
Big News
Births
Birthdays
Blood Drive
Give Blood
Books Needed
Bowling League

Break Away
Breakfast
Bridal Shower
Bring a Friend
Bring a Guest
Budget
Budget Meeting
Budget Planning
Building Fund
Bulletin Board
Bus
The Lord's Business
Business Meeting
By the Way . . .

Calendar
Calendar of Activities
Call to Worship
Camp
Campus News
Candlelight Service

Canned Food Drive
Caravan
Career Women
Care Groups
Catch the Spirit
C.E.
Celebrate!
Celebration!
Change of Date
Chancel Choir
Check It Out in
    the Library
Children
Children's Choir
Children's Church
Children's Department
Children's Ministry News
Choir
Choir Openings
Choir Practice
Christian Business
Christian Concert
Christian Education
Christian Service
Christmas
Christmas Eve
Christmas Program
Church
Church Budget
Church Bus
Church Cookbook
Church Council
Church Dinner
Church Family News
Church Library
Church Officers
Church Picnic
Church School
Churchtime
Church-wide Event
Church Workday
Circle of Concern
Classes
Class Officers
Clothing Needed
Coffee Break

Coming up . . .
Commissioning Service
Committees
Communion
Communion Worship
    Service
Concert
In Concert
Conference
Congratulations!
Convention
Core Groups
Counseling Center
Countdown to:
Couples' Retreat
Couples' Weekend
Covenant Groups
CPR Classes
Crusade
Crusaders

Date
Dated Material
Dates to Remember
Day Camp
Day Care
Daylight Savings Time
    Change
Day of Prayer
Day School
Deacon Board
Board of Deacons
Deaconesses
Deacons' Offering
Deadline
Ministry for the Deaf
Death
Dedication Service
Department
Dinner
Diplomas
Directories Now Available
Directory Changes
Directory Photos
Discipleship
Divorce Recovery Workshop

Dollars
Donation
Don't Forget

Easter
Easter Service
The Meaning of Easter
Elders
Electives
Engagement
Enrichment
Enrollment Time
Enroll Now
Envelopes
Equipping for the
    Ministry
Eucharist
Evangelism
Events
Exercise Class

Fall
Fall Retreat
Family Camp
Family Camping
Family Focus
Family News
Family Night
Family Resource
    Center
Famine Relief
Farewell
Father/Daughter
    Retreat
Father/Son Retreat
Father's Day
Fellowship
Film Series
Finances
Financial Report
Flowers
Focus
Food Bank Ministry
Food for the Hungry
Football
For the Entire Family

For the Record
Free
From the Desk of . . .
From the Pastor
Fruit of the Spirit
Fund

General Fund
Get Involved!
Get Well
Give Blood
Give Life
Give Thanks
God Answers Prayer
God Is Love
Golf
Good-bye . . .
Good Friday
Good News!
Gospel Singers
Graduation
Our Graduates
Grandparents
Guest Musicians
Guest Speaker

Hallelujah!
Halloween Party
Handicapped Parking
Happy Birthday!
Harvest Festival
Have You
   Considered This?
Have You Heard?
Have You Seen?
HELP!
Helping Hands
Help Needed
Help Wanted
Hey, Kids!
Home Bible Study
Homecoming
Hospital Ministry
In the Hospital
Host Committee
Hotline

Housing Needed
HURRY!
Hymns

Ice Cream Social
Important!
Important Message
Important Note:
Important! Please Read!
Infant Dedication
Ingathering Celebration
In Memory Of . . .
Inner-city Ministry
Invitation
It's Not Too Late

Join the Choir
Join Us
Jog-a-Thon
Jubilee
Junior Highlights
July 4th
Just a Note

Kick Off!
Kid's Klub
Kid's Korner
King's Business
King's Kids
Martin Luther King's
   Birthday
Koinonia

Labor of Love
Ladies:
Ladies Bible Study
Last Supper
The Latest!
Lay Ministers
Lent
Let's Get Acquainted
Letters from the
   Mission Field
Library
Lincoln's Birthday

Literature Table
Living Christmas Tree
The Logos
The Lord's Supper
Lost:
Lost & Found
Love Offering
Lunch
Luncheon

Mail
Make Plans
Maranatha
Mark Your Calendar
Marriage Encounter
Marriage Enrichment
   Weekend
Media Center
Meditation
Meeting
Meet the Candidates
Members
Membership Class
Memo:
Memorial Service
Men's Bible Study
Men's Fellowship
Men's Prayer Breakfast
Merry Christmas
Message
Midweek Meetings
Milestones
Ministry of
   Encouragement
Ministry Team
Miracles!
Our Mission
Our Missionaries
Mission Banquet
Mission Emphasis
   Week
Mission News
Missions
Monthly Meeting
Mom's Time Out
Mother/Daughter
   Retreat

Mother/Son Retreat
Mother's Day
Movie Night
Music
Music Ministry

Neighborhood Bible Study
New!
New Addresses
New Arrivals
New Elders
New Members' Class
New Officers
News & Notes
News Flash!
Newsletter
News of Note:
Newspaper Recycling
New Testament
    Classes
New to Our Family
Happy New Year!
Night Watch
Nominating Committee
Note!
Notes of Interest
Notice
Nursery News
Nursery Workers
Nursing Home Residents

Offering
Old Testament
Classes
Oops! We Goofed . . .
Open House Week
Opportunities
Opportunities for
    Growth
Ordination Service
Our Sympathy
Outlook:
Outreach

Pancake Breakfast
Paper Drive

Parenting Seminar
Passover
Passover Meal
Pastoral Staff
From the Pastor
From the Pastor's Pen
Pastor's Class
The Pastor's Column
Pastor's Notes
The Pastor's Page
Pastor's Perspective
Peace
Pentecost
People in the News
Phone
Picnic
Plan Ahead
Plan Now to Attend
PLEASE!
Please Return
Please Pray
Pledges
Potluck
Praise!
Praise the Lord!
Prayer Breakfast
Prayer Cells
Prayer Chain
Prayer Meeting
Prayer Partners
Prayer Requests
Prelude
Premarital Counseling
Preregistration
Presented by . . .
Preview
Prison Ministry
Progressive Dinner
Promotion Sunday
PSSST!
Put these Dates on
    Your Calendar

Radio Ministry
Rally
Rally Day
Red Cross

Registration Form
Relationships
Rejoice
Remember in Prayer
Reminder
Renewal
Rescue Mission
Reservations
Resource Center
Resurrection
Retreat
Roundup Sunday

Sabbath
Salvation
Sanctuary Flowers
Schedule
Scholarships
Scholarship Fund
See You Sunday!
Seminar
A Seminar for . . .
Senior Citizens
Senior Saints
Sermon Notes
Sermon Topics
Service Attendance
Servicemen's Center
Share
Share Your Faith
Short-Term Missions
Shut-ins
Sign Up
Singles' Spot
Singles' Study
Singspiration
Sing Unto the Lord
Small Groups
Sneak Preview
Soccer
Social Concern
Softball League
Something to
    Think About
Special Education
Special Events
Special Music

92

Special Need
Special Notice
Special Offering
Special Film
Special Gifts
Spiritual Emphasis Week
Spotlight
Spread the Word
Spring
Spring Fling
Sponsors Needed
Staff Anniversary
Staff Meeting
Staff Retreat
Steak Fry
Stewardship
Still in Need
Summer
Sunday
This Sunday
Sunday's Decisions
Sunday Evening
    Fellowship
Sunday Evening Service
Sunday Morning
Sunday Schedule
Sunday School
    Attendance
Sunday School Staff
Sunday's Statistics
Sunrise Service
Support Group
Support Group Meeting
Sweetheart Banquet

Take Note!
Tape Library
Tapes for Your
    Spiritual Growth

Teach a Child
Teacher of the Month
Teachers' Meeting
Teacher Training
Teen Missions
Testimony
Testimony Time
Thanksgiving
Thank You!
Thanks Offering
Thank You for Praying
Think About It!
This Week
Thot:
Thought:
Through the Bible
Time
Tithe
Tithes and Offerings
Today:
Toys Are Needed
Transportation Needed
Treasurer's Report
Training Program
Trustees
TV Worth Watching

Upcoming
Update
Ushers Are Needed

Vacation Bible School
Valentine's Day
VBS
VBS Rally
Video Series
Our Vision
Visitation
Volunteers Needed

Walk-a-Thon
Washington's Birthday
Weddings
Week at a Glance
Weekend Project
Weekend Retreat
Weekend Schedule
Weekly Schedule
We Have Called . . .
Welcome!
Welcome Home!
We Need Help!
We Need YOU!
We Still Need Workers
What's New?
Wheelchair Ministry
While You Were Out . . .
Winter
Wisdom
With Sympathy
Women's Bible Study
Women's Ministry
Women's Missionary
    Society
Woman's Retreat
Words of Wisdom
World Evangelism
World Outreach
Work Day
Work Project
Worship
Worship Committee
Worship Service

Yes!
Youth
Youth Choir
Youth Group
Youth News
Youth Nite
Youth Service

Days and Months

Saturday
Sunday
Monday
Tuesday
Wednesday
Thursday
Friday

January
February
March
April
May
June
July
August
September
October
November
December

Age Levels

Babyland
Nursery
Toddlers

Two-Year-Olds
Twos and Threes
Three-Year-Olds
Threes and Fours
Four-Year-Olds
Fours and Fives
Five-Year-Olds
Early Childhood
Children
Pre-K
Kindergarten
First Grade
Second Grade
Third Grade
Fourth Grade
Fifth Grade
Sixth Grade
Seventh Grade
Eighth Grade
Ninth Grade
Tenth Grade
Eleventh Grade
Twelfth Grade
Elementary
Primary
Junior
Junior High
Middler
Middle High

Mid-High
Senior High
College
College/Career
Young Adults
Young Marrieds
Singles
Adults
Seniors

Staff Positions

Administrator
Assistant Pastor
Associate Pastor
Bishop
Children's Director
Children's Minister
Church Administrator
Church Business
Administrator
Church Secretary
Clergy
Counselor
DCE
Deacon
Director of Christian
Education
Family Minister

Groundskeeper
Host
Hostess
Interim Pastor
Intern
Janitor
Lay Leader
Librarian
Maintenance
Minister
Minister of
Evangelism
Minister of Music
Minister of Visitation
Minister of Youth
Music Minister
Nursery Coordinator
Overseer
Pastor
Pastor Emeritus
Pastor of Visitation
Pulpit Committee
Secretary
Senior Pastor

Adult Fellowship
Advancement Sunday
Advent
Aerobics
Afterglow
Agape Love
All Are Welcome
All-Church Picnic
Also . . .
Ambassadors
And . . .

And the Lord Added
   to His Church
Announcements
Anniversaries
At Home and Abroad
Attendance
Attention, Men
Attention, Parents
Attention, Women
Awards Banquet

Babies
Baby Shower
Back to School
Backyard Bible Study
Bake Sale
Banquet
Baptism Service
Barbecue
Baseball
Basketball
Benevolence Fund
Bereans
Bible School
Bible Study
Big News
Births
Birthdays
Blood Drive
Give Blood
Books Needed
Bowling League
Break Away
Breakfast
Bridal Shower
Bring a Friend
Bring a Guest
Budget
Budget Meeting
Budget Planning
Building Fund
Bulletin Board
Bus

The Lord's Business
Business Meeting
By the Way . . .

Calendar
Calendar of Activities
Call to Worship
Camp
Campus News
Candlelight Service
Canned Food Drive
Caravan
Career Women
Care Groups
Catch the Spirit
C.E.
Celebrate!
Celebration!
Change of Date
Chancel Choir
Check It Out in the Library
Children
Children's Choir
Children's Church
Children's Department
Children's Ministry News
Choir
Choir Openings
Choir Practice
Christian Business
Christian Concert
Christian Education

Christian Service
Christmas
Christmas Eve
Christmas Program
Church
Church Budget
Church Bus
Church Cookbook
Church Council
Church Dinner
Church Family News
Church Library
Church Officers
Church Picnic
Church School
Churchtime
Church-wide Event
Church Workday
Circle of Concern
Classes
Class Officers
Clothing Needed
Coffee Break
Coming up . . .
Commissioning Service
Committees
Communion
Communion Worship Service
Concert
In Concert
Conference
Congratulations!

Convention
Core Groups
Counseling Center
Countdown to:
Couples' Retreat
Couples' Weekend
Covenant Groups
CPR Classes
Crusade
Crusaders

Date
Dated Material
Dates to Remember
Day Camp
Day Care
Daylight Savings Time Change
Day of Prayer
Day School
Deacon Board
Board of Deacons
Deaconesses
Deacons' Offering
Deadline
Ministry for the Deaf
Death
Dedication Service
Department
Dinner
Diplomas
Directories Now Available
Directory Changes

Directory Photos
Discipleship
Divorce Recovery Workshop
Dollars
Donation
Don't Forget

Easter
Easter Service
The Meaning of Easter
Elders
Electives
Engagement
Enrichment
Enrollment Time
Enroll Now
Envelopes
Equipping for the Ministry
Eucharist
Evangelism
Events
Exercise Class

Fall
Fall Retreat
Family Camp
Family Camping
Family Focus
Family News
Family Night
Family Resource Center
Famine Relief

Farewell
Father/Daughter Retreat
Father/Son Retreat
Father's Day
Fellowship
Film Series
Finances
Financial Report
Flowers
Focus
Food Bank Ministry
Food for the Hungry
Football
For the Entire Family
For the Record
Free
From the Desk of . . .
From the Pastor
Fruit of the Spirit
Fund

General Fund
Get Involved!
Get Well
Give Blood
Give Life
Give Thanks
God Answers Prayer
God Is Love
Golf
Good-bye . . .
Good Friday

Good News!
Gospel Singers
Graduation
Our Graduates
Grandparents
Guest Musicians
Guest Speaker

Hallelujah!
Halloween Party
Handicapped Parking
Happy Birthday!
Harvest Festival
Have You Considered This?
Have You Heard?
Have You Seen?
HELP!
Helping Hands
Help Needed
Help Wanted
Hey, Kids!
Home Bible Study
Homecoming
Hospital Ministry
In the Hospital
Host Committee
Hotline
Housing Needed
HURRY!
Hymns

Ice Cream Social

Important!
Important Message
Important Note:
Important! Please Read!
Infant Dedication
Ingathering Celebration
In Memory Of . . .
Inner-city Ministry
Invitation
It's Not Too Late

Join the Choir
Join Us
Jog-a-Thon
Jubilee
Junior Highlights
July 4th
Just a Note

Kick Off!
Kid's Klub
Kid's Korner
King's Business
King's Kids
Martin Luther King's Birthday
Koinonia

Labor of Love
Ladies:
Ladies Bible Study
Last Supper
The Latest!
Lay Ministers

Lent
Let's Get Acquainted
Letters from the Mission Field
Library
Lincoln's Birthday
Literature Table
Living Christmas Tree
The Logos
The Lord's Supper
Lost:
Lost & Found
Love Offering
Lunch
Luncheon

Mail
Make Plans
Maranatha
Mark Your Calendar
Marriage Encounter
Marriage Enrichment
    Weekend
Media Center
Meditation
Meeting
Meet the Candidates
Members
Membership Class
Memo:
Memorial Service
Men's Bible Study
Men's Fellowship

Men's Prayer Breakfast
Merry Christmas
Message
Midweek Meetings
Milestones
Ministry of
    Encouragement
Ministry Team
Miracles!
Our Mission
Our Missionaries
Mission Banquet
Mission Emphasis Week
Mission News
Missions
Monthly Meeting
Mom's Time Out
Mother/Daughter Retreat
Mother/Son Retreat
Mother's Day
Movie Night
Music
Music Ministry

Neighborhood Bible Study
New!
New Addresses
New Arrivals
New Elders
New Members' Class
New Officers
News & Notes

News Flash!
Newsletter
News of Note:
Newspaper Recycling
New Testament Classes
New to Our Family
Happy New Year!
Night Watch
Nominating Committee
Note!
Notes of Interest
Notice
Nursery News
Nursery Workers
Nursing Home Residents

Offering
Old Testament Classes
Oops! We Goofed . . .
Open House Week
Opportunities
Opportunities for Growth
Ordination Service
Our Sympathy
Outlook:
Outreach

Pancake Breakfast
Paper Drive
Parenting Seminar
Passover
Passover Meal

Pastoral Staff
From the Pastor
From the Pastor's Pen
Pastor's Class
The Pastor's Column
Pastor's Notes
The Pastor's Page
Pastor's Perspective
Peace
Pentecost
People in the News
Phone
Picnic
Plan Ahead
Plan Now to Attend
PLEASE!
Please Return
Please Pray
Pledges
Potluck
Praise!
Praise the Lord!
Prayer Breakfast
Prayer Cells
Prayer Chain
Prayer Meeting
Prayer Partners
Prayer Requests
Prelude
Premarital Counseling
Preregistration
Presented by . . .

Preview
Prison Ministry
Progressive Dinner
Promotion Sunday
PSSST!
Put these Dates on Your
	Calendar

Radio Ministry
Rally
Rally Day
Red Cross
Registration Form
Relationships
Rejoice
Remember in Prayer
Reminder
Renewal
Rescue Mission
Reservations
Resource Center
Resurrection
Retreat
Roundup Sunday

Sabbath
Salvation
Sanctuary Flowers
Schedule
Scholarships
Scholarship Fund
See You Sunday!

Seminar
A Seminar for . . .
Senior Citizens
Senior Saints
Sermon Notes
Sermon Topics
Service Attendance
Servicemen's Center
Share
Share Your Faith
Short-Term Missions
Shut-ins
Sign Up
Singles' Spot
Singles' Study
Singspiration
Sing Unto the Lord
Small Groups
Sneak Preview
Soccer
Social Concern
Softball League
Something to Think About
Special Education
Special Events
Special Music
Special Need
Special Notice
Special Offering
Special Film
Special Gifts
Spiritual Emphasis Week

Spotlight
Spread the Word
Spring
Spring Fling
Sponsors Needed
Staff Anniversary
Staff Meeting
Staff Retreat
Steak Fry
Stewardship
Still in Need
Summer
Sunday
This Sunday
Sunday's Decisions
Sunday Evening Fellowship
Sunday Evening Service
Sunday Morning
Sunday Schedule
Sunday School Attendance
Sunday School Staff
Sunday's Statistics
Sunrise Service
Support Group
Support Group Meeting
Sweetheart Banquet

Take Note!
Tape Library
Tapes for Your Spiritual Growth
Teach a Child
Teacher of the Month

Teachers' Meeting
Teacher Training
Teen Missions
Testimony
Testimony Time
Thanksgiving
Thank You!
Thanks Offering
Thank You for Praying
Think About It!
This Week
Thot:
Thought:
Through the Bible
Time
Tithe
Tithes and Offerings
Today:
Toys Are Needed
Transportation Needed
Treasurer's Report
Training Program
Trustees
TV Worth Watching

Upcoming
Update
Ushers Are Needed

Vacation Bible School
Valentine's Day
VBS

VBS Rally
Video Series
Our Vision
Visitation
Volunteers Needed

Walk-a-Thon
Washington's Birthday
Weddings
Week at a Glance
Weekend Project
Weekend Retreat
Weekend Schedule
Weekly Schedule
We Have Called . . .
Welcome!
Welcome Home!
We Need Help!
We Need YOU!
We Still Need Workers
What's New?
Wheelchair Ministry
While You Were Out . . .

Winter
Wisdom
With Sympathy
Women's Bible Study
Women's Ministry
Women's Missionary Society
Woman's Retreat
Words of Wisdom
World Evangelism
World Outreach
Work Day
Work Project
Worship
Worship Committee
Worship Service

Yes!
Youth
Youth Choir
Youth Group
Youth News
Youth Nite
Youth Service

156 BIBLE PASSAGES

Wisdom from God's Word can make a great "Thought for the Week" for your bulletin.

These popular verses have been printed in both the King James Version and *The New International Bible* version. The verses are listed in the order in which they appear in the Bible. A convenient topical index appears at the end of this section.

The King James version:

Ye are the children of the Lord your God.

Deuteronomy 14:1a

But know that the Lord hath set apart him that is godly for himself: the Lord will hear when I call unto him.

Psalm 4:3

But let all those that put their trust in thee rejoice: let them ever shout for joy, because thou defendest them: let them also that love thy name be joyful in thee.

Psalm 5:11

He maketh me to lie down in green pastures: he leadeth me beside the still waters. He restoreth my soul: he leadeth me in the paths of righteousness for his name's sake.

Psalm 23:2,3

Wait on the Lord: be of good courage, and he shall strengthen thine heart: wait, I say, on the Lord.

Psalm 27:14

The Lord is their strength, and he is the saving strength of his anointed.

Psalm 28:8

The Lord will give strength unto his people; the Lord will bless his people with peace.

Psalm 29:11

Be of good courage, and he shall strengthen your heart, all ye that hope in the Lord.

Psalm 31:24

Many sorrows shall be to the wicked: but he that trusteth in the Lord, mercy shall compass him about.

Psalm 32:10

Delight thyself also in the Lord; and he shall give thee the desires of thine heart. Commit thy way unto the Lord; trust also in him; and he shall bring it to pass.

Psalm 37:4,5

Cease from anger, and forsake wrath: fret not thyself in any wise to do evil.

Psalm 37:8

Blessed is that man that maketh the Lord his trust, and respecteth not the proud, nor such as turn aside to lies.

Psalm 40:4

Sing praises to God, sing praises: sing praises unto our King, sing praises.

Psalm 47:6

Wash me throughly from mine iniquity, and cleanse me from my sin.

Psalm 51:2

The fool hath said in his heart, There is no God.

Psalm 53:1a

Cast thy burden upon the Lord, and he shall sustain thee: he shall never suffer the righteous to be moved.

Psalm 55:22

O bless our God, ye people, and make the voice of his praise to be heard.

Psalm 66:8

My lips shall greatly rejoice when I sing unto thee; and my soul, which thou hast redeemed.

Psalm 71:23

Help us, O God of our salvation, for the glory of thy name: and deliver us, and purge away our sins, for thy name's sake.

Psalm 79:9

Declare his glory among the heathen, his wonders among all people.

Psalm 96:3

The heavens declare his righteousness, and all the people see his glory.

Psalm 97:6

Make a joyful noise unto the Lord, all the earth: make a loud noise, and rejoice, and sing praise.

Psalm 98:4

Exalt ye the Lord our God, and worship at his footstool; for he is holy.

Psalm 99:5

As far as the east is from the west, so far hath he removed our transgressions from us.

Psalm 103:12

I will sing unto the Lord as long as I live: I will sing praise to my God while I have my being.

Psalm 104:33

Seek the Lord, and his strength: seek his face evermore.

Psalm 105:4

I love the Lord, because he hath heard my voice and my supplications.

Psalm 116:1

This is the day which the Lord hath made; we will rejoice and be glad in it.

Psalm 118:24

Blessed art thou, O Lord: teach me thy statutes.

Psalm 119:12

Happy is that people, that is in such a case: yea, happy is that people, whose God is the Lord.

Psalm 144:15

The Lord is nigh unto all them that call upon him, to all that call upon him, in truth.

Psalm 145:18

Happy is he that hath the God of Jacob for his help, whose hope is in the Lord his God.

Psalm 146:5

Let not mercy and truth forsake thee: bind them about thy neck; write them upon the table of thine heart.

Proverbs 3:3

Trust in the Lord with all thine heart; and lean not unto thine own understanding.

Proverbs 3:5

The fear of the Lord is to hate evil: pride, and arrogancy, and the evil way, and the froward mouth, do I hate.

Proverbs 8:13

The fear of the Lord is the beginning of wisdom: and the knowledge of the holy is understanding.

Proverbs 9:10

He that walketh uprightly walketh surely: but he that perverteth his ways shall be known.

Proverbs 10:9

The fear of the Lord prolongeth days: but the years of the wicked shall be shortened.

Proverbs 10:27

Lying lips are abomination to the Lord: but they that deal truly are his delight.

Proverbs 12:22

A soft answer turneth away wrath: but grievous words stir up anger.

Proverbs 15:1

Commit thy works unto the Lord, and thy thoughts shall be established.

Proverbs 16:3

By mercy and truth iniquity is purged: and by the fear of the Lord men depart from evil.

Proverbs 16:6

He that handleth a matter wisely shall find good: and whoso trusteth in the Lord, happy is he.

Proverbs 16:20

Better is the poor that walketh in his integrity, than he that is perverse in his lips, and is a fool.

Proverbs 19:1

Apply thine heart unto instruction, and thine ears to the words of knowledge.

Proverbs 23:12

Come now, and let us reason together, saith the Lord: though your sins be as scarlet, they shall be as white as snow; though they be red like crimson, they shall be as wool.

Isaiah 1:18

Behold, God is my salvation; I will trust, and not be afraid: for the Lord JEHOVAH is my strength and my song; he also is become my salvation.

Isaiah 12:2

And it shall come to pass, that before they call, I will answer; and while they are yet speaking, I will hear.

Isaiah 65:24

Blessed are the peacemakers: for they shall be called the children of God.

Matthew 5:9

Then shall the righteous shine forth as the sun in the kingdom of their Father. Who hath ears to hear, let him hear.

Matthew 13:43

And I say also unto thee, That thou art Peter, and upon this rock I will build my church; and the gates of hell shall not prevail against it.

Matthew 16:18

But it shall not be so among you: but whosoever will be great among you, let him be your minister.

Matthew 20:26

And all things, whatsoever ye shall ask in prayer, believing, ye shall receive.

Matthew 21:22

And this gospel of the kingdom shall be preached in all the world for a witness unto all nations; and then shall the end come.

Matthew 24:14

For this is my blood of the new testament, which is shed for many for the remission of sins.

Matthew 26:28

Go ye therefore, and teach all nations, baptizing them in the name of the Father, and of the Son, and of the Holy Ghost.

Matthew 28:19

Jesus said unto him, If thou canst believe, all things are possible to him that believeth.

Mark 9:23

And the gospel must first be published among all nations.

Mark 13:10

He that believeth and is baptized shall be saved; but he that believeth not shall be damned.

Mark 16:16

And Jesus answered and said unto him, Get thee behind me, Satan: for it is written, Thou shalt worship the Lord thy God, and him only shalt thou serve.

Luke 4:8

I came not to call the righteous, but sinners to repentance.

Luke 5:32

I say unto you, that likewise joy shall be in heaven over one sinner that repenteth, more than over ninety and nine just persons, which need no repentance.

Luke 15:7

He that is faithful in that which is least is faithful also in much: and he that is unjust in the least is unjust also in much.

Luke 16:10

And it is easier for heaven and earth to pass, than one tittle of the law to fail.

Luke 16:17

But as many as received him, to them gave he power to become the sons of God, even to them that believe on his name.

John 1:12

For God so loved the world, that he gave his only begotten Son, that whosoever believeth in him should not perish, but have everlasting life.

John 3:16

But the hour cometh, and now is, when the true worshippers shall worship the Father in spirit and in truth: for the Father seeketh such to worship him.

John 4:23

I am the living bread which came down from heaven: if any man eat of this bread, he shall live for ever: and the bread that I will give is my flesh, which I will give for the life of the world.

John 6:51

And ye shall know the truth, and the truth shall make you free.

John 8:32

If any man serve me, let him follow me; and where I am, there shall also my servant be: if any man serve me, him will my Father honour.

John 12:26

Ye call me Master and Lord: and ye say well; for so I am.

John 13:13

Jesus saith unto him, I am the way, the truth, and the life: no man cometh unto the Father, but by me.

John 14:6

If ye love me, keep my commandments.

John 14:15

And I will pray the Father, and he shall give you another Comforter, that he may abide with you for ever.

John 14:16

Therefore let all the house of Israel know assuredly, that God hath made that same Jesus, whom ye have crucified, both Lord and Christ.

Acts 2:36

Neither is there salvation in any other: for there is none other name under heaven given among men, whereby we must be saved.

Acts 4:12

And now why tarriest thou? arise, and be baptized, and wash away thy sins, calling on the name of the Lord.

Acts 22:16

Among whom are ye also the called of Jesus Christ.

Romans 1:6

Grace to you and peace from God our Father, and the Lord Jesus Christ.

Romans 1:7b

For all have sinned, and come short of the glory of God.

Romans 3:23

Therefore being justified by faith, we have peace with God through our Lord Jesus Christ.

Romans 5:1

For the wages of sin is death; but the gift of God is eternal life through Jesus Christ our Lord.

Romans 6:23

For to be carnally minded is death; but to be spiritually minded is life and peace.

Romans 8:6

For as many as are led by the Spirit of God, they are the sons of God.

Romans 8:14

And we know that all things work together for good to them that love God, to them who are the called according to his purpose.

Romans 8:28

For I am persuaded, that neither death, nor life, nor angels, nor principalities, nor powers, nor things present, nor things to come, Nor height, nor depth, nor any other creature, shall be able to separate us from the love of God, which is in Christ Jesus our Lord.

Romans 8:38,39

Whose are the fathers, and of whom as concerning the flesh Christ came, who is over all, God blessed for ever. Amen.

Romans 9:5

We then that are strong ought to bear the infirmities of the weak, and not to please ourselves.

Romans 15:1

Now the God of patience and consolation grant you to be likeminded one toward another according to Christ Jesus: That ye may with one mind and one mouth glorify God, even the Father of our Lord Jesus Christ.

Romans 15:5,6

Now the God of hope fill you with all joy and peace in believing, that ye may abound in hope, through the power of the Holy Ghost.

Romans 15:13

Now the God of peace be with you all. Amen.

Romans 15:33

That your faith should not stand in the wisdom of men, but in the power of God.

1 Corinthians 2:5

For we are labourers together with God: ye are God's husbandry, ye are God's building.

1 Corinthians 3:9

Know ye not that ye are the temple of God, and that the Spirit of God dwelleth in you?

1 Corinthians 3:16

And such were some of you: but ye are washed, but ye are sanctified, but ye are justified in the name of the Lord Jesus, and by the Spirit of our God.

1 Corinthians 6:11

And God hath both raised up the Lord, and will also raise up us by his own power.

1 Corinthians 6:14

The cup of blessing which we bless, is it not the communion of the blood of Christ? The bread which we break, is it not the communion of the body of Christ? For we being many are one bread, and one body: for we are all partakers of that one bread.

1 Corinthians 10:16,17

Whether therefore ye eat, or drink, or whatsoever ye do, do all to the glory of God.

1 Corinthians 10:31

For as often as ye eat this bread, and drink this cup, ye do show the Lord's death till he come.

1 Corinthians 11:26

For by one Spirit are we all baptized into one body, whether we be Jews or Gentiles, whether we be bond or free; and have been all made to drink into one Spirit.

1 Corinthians 12:13

Awake to righteousness, and sin not; for some have not the knowledge of God: I speak this to your shame.

1 Corinthians 15:34

For we preach not ourselves, but Christ Jesus the Lord; and ourselves your servants for Jesus' sake.

2 Corinthians 4:5

For all things are for your sakes, that the abundant grace might through the thanksgiving of many redound to the glory of God.

2 Corinthians 4:15

Having therefore these promises, dearly beloved, let us cleanse ourselves from all filthiness of the flesh and spirit, perfecting holiness in the fear of God.

2 Corinthians 7:1

The grace of the Lord Jesus Christ, and the love of God, and the communion of the Holy Ghost, be with you all. Amen.

2 Corinthians 13:14

For as many of you as have been baptized into Christ have put on Christ.

Galatians 3:27

And because ye are sons, God hath sent forth the Spirit of his Son into your hearts, crying, Abba, Father.

Galatians 4:6

Wherefore thou art no more a servant, but a son; and if a son, then an heir of God through Christ.

Galatians 4:7

But the fruit of the Spirit is love, joy, peace, longsuffering, gentleness, goodness, faith, Meekness, temperance: against such there is no law.

Galatians 5:22,23

For he that soweth to his flesh shall of the flesh reap corruption; but he that soweth to the Spirit shall of the Spirit reap life everlasting.

Galatians 6:8

As we have therefore opportunity, let us do good unto all men, especially unto them who are of the household of faith.

Galatians 6:10

Having predestinated us unto the adoption of children by Jesus Christ to himself, according to the good pleasure of his will.

Ephesians 1:5

And hath put all things under his feet, and gave him to be the head over all things to the church, Which is his body, the fulness of him that filleth all in all.

Ephesians 1:22,23

For by grace are ye saved through faith; and that not of yourselves: it is the gift of God.

Ephesians 2:8

That he would grant you, according to the riches of his glory, to be strengthened with might by his Spirit in the inner man.

Ephesians 3:16

But unto every one of us is given grace according to the measure of the gift of Christ.

Ephesians 4:7

Be ye angry, and sin not: let not the sun go down upon your wrath.

Ephesians 4:26

And walk in love, as Christ also hath loved us, and hath given himself for us an offering and a sacrifice to God for a sweetsmelling savour.

Ephesians 5:2

For the husband is the head of the wife, even as Christ is the head of the church: and he is the saviour of the body.

Ephesians 5:23

Peace be to the brethren, and love with faith, from God the Father and the Lord Jesus Christ.

Ephesians 6:23

Rejoice in the Lord alway: and again I say, Rejoice.

Philippians 4:4

Be careful for nothing; but in every thing by prayer and supplication with thanksgiving let your requests be made known unto God.

Philippians 4:6

And the peace of God, which passeth all understanding, shall keep your hearts and minds through Christ Jesus.

Philippians 4:7

Buried with him in baptism, wherein also ye are risen with him through the faith of the operation of God, who hath raised him from the dead.

Colossians 2:12

But now ye also put off all these; anger, wrath, malice, blasphemy, filthy communication out of your mouth.

Colossians 3:8

And let the peace of God rule in your hearts, to the which also ye are called in one body; and be ye thankful.

Colossians 3:15

Continue in prayer, and watch in the same with thanksgiving.

Colossians 4:2

And the Lord make you to increase and abound in love one toward another, and toward all men, even as we do toward you.

1 Thessalonians 3:12

For God hath not appointed us to wrath, but to obtain salvation by our Lord Jesus Christ.

1 Thessalonians 5:9

Quench not the Spirit.

1 Thessalonians 5:19

Now the end of the commandment is charity out of a pure heart, and of a good conscience, and of faith unfeigned.

1 Timothy 1:5

I will therefore that men pray every where, lifting up holy hands, without wrath and doubting.

1 Timothy 2:8

Fight the good fight of faith, lay hold on eternal life, whereunto thou art also called, and hast professed a good profession before many witnesses.

1 Timothy 6:12

All scripture is given by inspiration of God, and is profitable for doctrine, for reproof, for correction, for instruction in righteousness: That the man of God may be perfect, throughly furnished unto all good works.

2 Timothy 3:16,17

Not by works of righteousness which we have done, but according to his mercy he saved us, by the washing of regeneration, and renewing of the Holy Ghost;

Titus 3:5

Let us therefore come boldly unto the throne of grace, that we may obtain mercy, and find grace to help in time of need.

Hebrews 4:16

For if we sin willfully after that we have received the knowledge of the truth, there remaineth no more sacrifice for sins.

Hebrews 10:26

Now the God of peace, that brought again from the dead our Lord Jesus, that great shepherd of the sheep, through the blood of the everlasting covenant, Make you perfect in every good work to do his will, working in you that which is wellpleasing in his sight, through Jesus Christ; to whom be glory for ever and ever. Amen.

Hebrews 13:20,21

Wherefore, my beloved brethren, let every man be swift to hear, slow to speak, slow to wrath.

James 1:19

Confess your faults one to another, and pray one for another, that ye may be healed. The effectual fervent prayer of a righteous man availeth much.

James 5:16

For Christ also hath once suffered for sins, the just for the unjust, that he might bring us to God, being put to death in the flesh, but quickened by the Spirit.

1 Peter 3:18

But the God of all grace, who hath called us unto his eternal glory by Christ Jesus, after that ye have suffered a while, make you perfect, stablish, strengthen, settle you. To him be glory and dominion for ever and ever. Amen.

1 Peter 5:10,11

Ye therefore, beloved, seeing ye know these things before, beware lest ye also, being led away with the error of the wicked, fall from your own stedfastness.

2 Peter 3:17

But if we walk in the light, as he is in the light, we have fellowship one with another, and the blood of Jesus Christ his Son cleanseth us from all sin.

1 John 1:7

And hereby we do know that we know him, if we keep his commandments.

1 John 2:3

Beloved, now are we the sons of God, and it doth not yet appear what we shall be: but we know that, when he shall appear, we shall be like him; for we shall see him as he is.

1 John 3:2

Beloved, let us love one another: for love is of God; and every one that loveth is born of God, and knoweth God.

1 John 4:7

Beloved, if God so loved us, we ought also to love one another.

1 John 4:11

Hereby know we that we dwell in him, and he in us, because he hath given us of his Spirit.

1 John 4:13

Whosoever shall confess that Jesus is the Son of God, God dwelleth in him, and he in God.

1 John 4:15

And we have known and believed the love that God hath to us. God is love; and he that dwelleth in love dwelleth in God, and God in him.

1 John 4:16

We love him, because he first loved us.

1 John 4:19

For whatsoever is born of God overcometh the world: and this is the victory that overcometh the world, even our faith.

1 John 5:4

These things have I written unto you that believe on the name of the Son of God; that ye may know that ye have eternal life, and that ye may believe on the name of the Son of God.

1 John 5:13

Behold, he cometh with clouds; and every eye shall see him, and they also which pierced him: and all kindreds of the earth shall wail because of him. Even so, Amen.

Revelation 1:7

I am he that liveth, and was dead; and, behold, I am alive for evermore, Amen; and have the keys of hell and of death.

Revelation 1:18

The New International Bible version:

You are the children of the Lord your God.

Deuteronomy 14:1a

Know that the Lord has set apart the godly for himself; the Lord will hear when I call to him.

Psalm 4:3

But let all who take refuge in you be glad;
    let them ever sing for joy.
Spread your protection over them,
    that those who love your name may rejoice in you.

Psalm 5:11

He makes me lie down in green pastures,
he leads me beside quiet waters,
    he restores my soul.
He guides me in paths of righteousness
    for his name's sake.

Psalm 23:2,3

Wait for the Lord;
    be strong and take heart
    and wait for the Lord.

Psalm 27:14

The Lord is the strength of his people,
    a fortress of salvation for his anointed one.

Psalm 28:8

The Lord gives strength to his people;
    the Lord blesses his people with peace.

Psalm 29:11

Be strong and take heart,
    all you who hope in the Lord.
                Psalm 31:24

Many are the woes of the wicked,
    but the Lord's unfailing love
    surrounds the man who trusts in
him.
                Psalm 32:10

Delight yourself in the Lord
    and he will give you the desires of
your heart.
Commit your way to the Lord;
    trust in him and he will do this:
                Psalm 37:4,5

Refrain from anger and turn from
wrath;
    do not fret—it leads only to evil.
                Psalm 37:8

Blessed is the man
    who makes the Lord his trust,
who does not look to the proud,
    to those who turn aside to false
gods.
                Psalm 40:4

Sing praises to God, sing praises;
    sing praises to our King, sing
praises.
                Psalm 47:6

Wash away all my iniquity
    and cleanse me from my sin.
                Psalm 51:2

The fool says in his heart,
    "There is no God."
                Psalm 53:1a

Cast your cares on the Lord
    and he will sustain you;
    he will never let the righteous fall.
                Psalm 55:22

Praise our God, O peoples,
    let the sound of his praise be heard;
                Psalm 66:8

My lips will shout for joy
    when I sing praise to you—
    I, whom you have redeemed.
                Psalm 71:23

Help us, O God our Savior,
    for the glory of your name;
deliver us and atone for our sins
    for your name's sake.
                Psalm 79:9

Declare his glory among the nations,
    his marvelous deeds among all
peoples.
                Psalm 96:3

The heavens proclaim his
righteousness,
    and all the peoples see his glory.
                Psalm 97:6

Shout for joy to the Lord, all the earth,
    burst into jubilant song with music;
                Psalm 98:4

Exalt the Lord our God
    and worship at his footstool;
    he is holy.
                Psalm 99:5

As far as the east is from the west,
    so far has he removed our
transgressions from us.
                Psalm 103:12

I will sing to the Lord all my life;
    I will sing praise to my God as long
as I live.
                Psalm 104:33

Look to the Lord and his strength;
    seek his face always.
                Psalm 105:4

I love the Lord, for he heard my voice;
    he heard my cry for mercy.
                Psalm 116:1

This is the day the Lord has made;
    let us rejoice and be glad in it.
                Psalm 118:24

Praise be to you, O Lord;
    teach me your decrees.
                Psalm 119:12

Blessed are the people of whom this is
true;
    blessed are the people whose God is
the Lord.
                Psalm 144:15

The Lord is near to all who call on
him,
    to all who call on him in truth.
                Psalm 145:18

Blessed is he whose help is the God of
Jacob,
    whose hope is in the Lord his God.
                Psalm 146:5

Let love and faithfulness never leave
you; bind them around your neck,
write them on the tablet of your heart.
                Proverbs 3:3

Trust in the Lord with all your heart
and lean not on your own
understanding;
                Proverbs 3:5

To fear the Lord is to hate evil; I hate
pride and arrogance, evil behavior and
perverse speech.
                Proverbs 8:13

The fear of the Lord is the beginning of
wisdom, and knowledge of the Holy
One is understanding.
                Proverbs 9:10

The man of integrity walks securely,
but he who takes crooked paths will be
found out.
                Proverbs 10:9

The fear of the Lord adds length to life,
but the years of the wicked are cut
short.
                Proverbs 10:27

The Lord detests lying lips, but he
delights in men who are truthful.
                Proverbs 12:22

A gentle answer turns away wrath, but a harsh word stirs up anger.

Proverbs 15:1

Commit to the Lord whatever you do, and your plans will succeed.

Proverbs 16:3

Through love and faithfulness sin is atoned for; through the fear of the Lord a man avoids evil.

Proverbs 16:6

Whoever gives heed to instruction prospers, and blessed is he who trusts in the Lord.

Proverbs 16:20

Better a poor man whose walk is blameless than a fool whose lips are perverse.

Proverbs 19:1

Apply your heart to instruction and your ears to words of knowledge.

Proverbs 23:12

"Come now, let us reason together," says the Lord.
"Though your sins are like scarlet, they shall be as white as snow; though they are red as crimson, they shall be like wool."

Isaiah 1:18

Surely God is my salvation;
I will trust and not be afraid.
The Lord, the Lord, is my strength and my song;
he has become my salvation.

Isaiah 12:2

Before they call I will answer;
while they are still speaking I will hear.

Isaiah 65:24

Blessed are the peacemakers,
for they will be called sons of God.

Matthew 5:9

Then the righteous will shine like the sun in the kingdom of their Father. He who has ears, let him hear.

Matthew 13:43

And I tell you that you are Peter, and on this rock I will build my church, and the gates of Hades will not overcome it.

Matthew 16:18

Not so with you. Instead, whoever wants to become great among you must be your servant.

Matthew 20:26

If you believe, you will receive whatever you ask for in prayer.

Matthew 21:22

And this gospel of the kingdom will be preached in the whole world as a testimony to all nations, and then the end will come.

Matthew 24:14

This is my blood of the covenant, which is poured out for many for the forgiveness of sins.

Matthew 26:28

Therefore go and make disciples of all nations, baptizing them in the name of the Father and of the Son and of the Holy Spirit.

Matthew 28:19

"'If you can'?" said Jesus. "Everything is possible for him who believes."

Mark 9:23

And the gospel must first be preached to all nations.

Mark 13:10

Whoever believes and is baptized will be saved, but whoever does not believe will be condemned.

Mark 16:16

Jesus answered, "It is written: 'Worship the Lord your God and serve him only.'"

Luke 4:8

I have not come to call the righteous, but sinners to repentance.

Luke 5:32

I tell you that in the same way there is more rejoicing in heaven over one sinner who repents than over ninety-nine righteous persons who do not need to repent.

Luke 15:7

Whoever can be trusted with very little can also be trusted with much, and whoever is dishonest with very little will also be dishonest with much.

Luke 16:10

It is easier for heaven and earth to disappear than for the least stroke of a pen to drop out of the Law.

Luke 16:17

Yet to all who received him, to those who believed in his name, he gave the right to become children of God.

John 1:12

For God so loved the world that he gave his one and only Son, that whoever believes in him shall not perish but have eternal life.

John 3:16

Yet a time is coming and has now come when the true worshipers will worship the Father in spirit and truth, for they are the kind of worshipers the Father seeks.

John 4:23

I am the living bread that came down from heaven. If a man eats of this bread, he will live forever. This bread is my flesh, which I will give for the life of the world.

John 6:51

Then you will know the truth, and the truth will set you free.

John 8:32

Whoever serves me must follow me; and where I am, my servant also will be. My Father will honor the one who serves me.

John 12:26

You call me 'Teacher' and 'Lord,' and rightly so, for that is what I am.

John 13:13

Jesus answered, "I am the way and the truth and the life. No one comes to the Father except through me.

John 14:6

If you love me, you will obey what I command.

John 14:15

And I will ask the Father, and he will give you another Counselor to be with you forever.

John 14:16

Therefore let all Israel be assured of this: God has made this Jesus, whom you crucified, both Lord and Christ.

Acts 2:36

Salvation is found in no one else, for there is no other name under heaven given to men by which we must be saved.

Acts 4:12

And now what are you waiting for? Get up, be baptized and wash your sins away, calling on his name.

Acts 22:16

And you also are among those who are called to belong to Jesus Christ.

Romans 1:6

Grace and peace to you from God our Father and from the Lord Jesus Christ.

Romans 1:7b

For all have sinned and fall short of the glory of God.

Romans 3:23

Therefore, since we have been justified through faith, we have peace with God through our Lord Jesus Christ.

Romans 5:1

For the wages of sin is death, but the gift of God is eternal life in Christ Jesus our Lord.

Romans 6:23

The mind of sinful man is death, but the mind controlled by the Spirit is life and peace.

Romans 8:6

Because those who are led by the Spirit of God are sons of God.

Romans 8:14

The Spirit himself testifies with our spirit that we are God's children.

Romans 8:16

And we know that in all things God works for the good of those who love him, who have been called according to his purpose.

Romans 8:28

For I am convinced that neither death nor life, neither angels nor demons, neither the present nor the future, nor any powers, neither height nor depth, nor anything else in all creation, will be able to separate us from the love of God that is in Christ Jesus our Lord.

Romans 8:38,39

Theirs are the patriarchs, and from them is traced the human ancestry of Christ, who is God over all, forever praised! Amen.

Romans 9:5

We who are strong ought to bear with the failings of the weak and not to please ourselves.

Romans 15:1

May the God who gives endurance and encouragement give you a spirit of unity among yourselves as you follow Christ Jesus, so that with one heart and mouth you may glorify the God and Father of our Lord Jesus Christ.

Romans 15:5,6

May the God of hope fill you with all joy and peace as you trust in him, so that you may overflow with hope by the power of the Holy Spirit.

Romans 15:13

The God of peace be with you all. Amen.

Romans 15:33

So that your faith might not rest on men's wisdom, but on God's power.

1 Corinthians 2:5

For we are God's fellow workers; you are God's field, God's building.

1 Corinthians 3:9

Don't you know that you yourselves are God's temple and that God's Spirit lives in you?

1 Corinthians 3:16

And that is what some of you were. But you were washed, you were sanctified, you were justified in the name of the Lord Jesus Christ and by the Spirit of our God.

1 Corinthians 6:11

By his power God raised the Lord from the dead, and he will raise us also.

1 Corinthians 6:14

Is not the cup of thanksgiving for which we give thanks a participation in the blood of Christ? And is not the bread that we break a participation in the body of Christ? Because there is one loaf, we, who are many are one body, for we all partake of the one loaf.

1 Corinthians 10:16,17

So whether you eat or drink or whatever you do, do it all for the glory of God.

1 Corinthians 10:31

For whenever you eat this bread and drink this cup, you proclaim the Lord's death until he comes.

1 Corinthians 11:26

For we were all baptized by one Spirit into one body—whether Jews or Greeks, slave or free—and we were all given the one Spirit to drink.

1 Corinthians 12:13

Come back to your senses as you ought, and stop sinning; for there are some who are ignorant of God—I say this to your shame.

1 Corinthians 15:34

For we do not preach ourselves, but Jesus Christ as Lord, and ourselves as your servants for Jesus' sake.

2 Corinthians 4:5

All this is for your benefit, so that the grace that is reaching more and more people may cause thanksgiving to overflow to the glory of God.

2 Corinthians 4:15

Since we have these promises, dear friends, let us purify ourselves from everything that contaminates body and spirit, perfecting holiness out of reverence for God.

2 Corinthians 7:1

May the grace of the Lord Jesus Christ, and the love of God, and the fellowship of the Holy Spirit be with you all.

2 Corinthians 13:14

For all of you who were baptized into Christ have been clothed with Christ.

Galatians 3:27

Because you are sons, God sent the Spirit of his Son into our hearts, the Spirit who calls out, "*Abba*, Father."

Galatians 4:6

So you are no longer a slave, but a son; and since you are a son, God has made you also an heir.

Galatians 4:7

But the fruit of the Spirit is love, joy, peace, patience, kindness, goodness, faithfulness, gentleness and self-control. Against such things there is no law.

Galatians 5:22,23

The one who sows to please his sinful nature, from that nature will reap destruction; the one who sows to please the Spirit, from the Spirit will reap eternal life.

Galatians 6:8

Therefore, as we have opportunity, let us do good to all people, especially to those who belong to the family of believers.

Galatians 6:10

He predestined us to be adopted as his sons through Jesus Christ, in accordance with his pleasure and will.

Ephesians 1:5

And God placed all things under his feet and appointed him to be head over everything for the church, which is his body, the fullness of him who fills everything in every way.

Ephesians 1:22,23

For it is by grace you have been saved, through faith—and this not from yourselves, it is the gift of God.

Ephesians 2:8

I pray that out of his glorious riches he may strengthen you with power through his Spirit in your inner being.

Ephesians 3:16

But to each one of us grace has been given as Christ apportioned it.

Ephesians 4:7

In your anger do not sin: Do not let the sun go down while you are still angry.

Ephesians 4:26

And live a life of love, just as Christ loved us and gave himself up for us as a fragrant offering and sacrifice to God.

Ephesians 5:2

For the husband is the head of the wife as Christ is the head of the church, his body, of which he is the Savior.

Ephesians 5:23

Peace to the brothers, and love with faith from God the Father and the Lord Jesus Christ.

Ephesians 6:23

Rejoice in the Lord always, I will say it again: Rejoice!

Philippians 4:4

Do not be anxious about anything, but in everything, by prayer and petition, with thanksgiving, present your requests to God.

Philippians 4:6

And the peace of God, which transcends all understanding, will guard your hearts and your minds in Christ Jesus.

Philippians 4:7

Having been buried with him in baptism and raised with him through your faith in the power of God, who raised him from the dead.

Colossians 2:12

But now you must rid yourselves of all such things as these: anger, rage, malice, slander, and filthy language from your lips.

Colossians 3:8

Let the peace of Christ rule in your hearts, since as members of one body you were called to peace. And be thankful.

Colossians 3:15

Devote yourselves to prayer, being watchful and thankful.

Colossians 4:2

May the Lord make your love increase and overflow for each other and for everyone else, just as ours does for you.

1 Thessalonians 3:12

For God did not appoint us to suffer wrath but to receive salvation through our Lord Jesus Christ.

1 Thessalonians 5:9

Do not put out the Spirit's fire.

1 Thessalonians 5:19

The goal of this command is love, which comes from a pure heart and a good conscience and a sincere faith.

1 Timothy 1:5

I want men everywhere to lift up holy hands in prayer, without anger or disputing.

1 Timothy 2:8

Fight the good fight of the faith. Take hold of the eternal life to which you were called when you made your good confession in the presence of many witnesses.

1 Timothy 6:12

All Scripture is God-breathed and is useful for teaching, rebuking, correcting and training in righteousness, so that the man of God may be thoroughly equipped for every good work.

2 Timothy 3:16,17

He saved us, not because of righteous things we had done, but because of his mercy. He saved us through the washing of rebirth and renewal by the Holy Spirit.

Titus 3:5

Let us then approach the throne of grace with confidence, so that we may receive mercy and find grace to help us in our time of need.

Hebrews 4:16

If we deliberately keep on sinning after we have received the knowledge of the truth, no sacrifice for sins is left.

Hebrews 10:26

May the God of peace, who through the blood of the eternal covenant brought back from the dead our Lord Jesus, that great Shepherd of the sheep, equip you with everything good for doing his will, and may he work in us what is pleasing to him, through Jesus Christ, to whom be glory for ever and ever. Amen.

Hebrews 13:20,21

My dear brothers, take note of this: Everyone should be quick to listen, slow to speak and slow to become angry.

James 1:19

Therefore confess your sins to each other and pray for each other so that you may be healed. The prayer of a righteous man is powerful and effective.

James 5:16

For Christ died for sins once for all, the righteous for the unrighteous, to bring you to God. He was put to death in the body but made alive by the Spirit.

1 Peter 3:18

And the God of all grace, who called you to his eternal glory in Christ, after you have suffered a little while, will himself restore you and make you strong, firm and steadfast. To him be the power for ever and ever. Amen.

1 Peter 5:10,11

Therefore, dear friends, since you already know this, be on your guard so that you may not be carried away by the error of lawless men and fall from your secure position.

2 Peter 3:17

But if we walk in the light, as he is in the light, we have fellowship with one another, and the blood of Jesus, his Son, purifies us from every sin.

1 John 1:7

We know that we have come to know him if we obey his commands.

1 John 2:3

Dear friends, now we are children of God, and what we will be has not yet been made known. But we know that when he appears, we shall be like him, for we shall see him as he is.

1 John 3:2

Dear friends, let us love one another, for love comes from God. Everyone who loves has been born of God and knows God.

1 John 4:7

Dear friends, since God so loved us, we also ought to love one another.

1 John 4:11

We know that we live in him and he in us, because he has given us of his Spirit.

1 John 4:13

If anyone acknowledges that Jesus is the Son of God, God lives in him and he in God.

1 John 4:15

And so we know and rely on the love God has for us.

1 John 4:16

We love because he first loved us.

1 John 4:19

For everyone born of God has overcome the world. This is the victory that has overcome the world, even our faith.

1 John 5:4

I write these things to you who believe in the name of the Son of God so that you may know that you have eternal life.

1 John 5:13

Look, he is coming with the clouds,
    and every eye will see him,
even those who pierced him;
    and all the peoples of the earth will mourn
    because of him.
So shall it be! Amen.

Revelation 1:7

I am the Living One; I was dead, and behold I am alive for ever and ever! And I hold the keys of death and Hades.

Revelation 1:18

TOPICAL INDEX TO THIS SECTION

Ablution   Pss. 51:2; 79:9; Prov. 16:6; 1 Cor. 6:11

Anger   Ps. 37:8; Prov. 15:1; Jas. 1:19; Eph. 4:26; Col. 3:8

Apostasy   Heb. 10:26; 2 Pet. 3:17

Assurance   Ps. 4:3; Rom. 1:6

Atheism   Ps. 53:1a

Baptism   Mark 16:16; Acts 22:16; 1 Cor. 12:13; Gal. 3:27; Col. 2:12

Benedictions   Rom. 1:7b; 15:5,6,13,33; 2 Cor. 13:14; Eph. 6:23; Heb. 13:20,21; 1 Pet. 5:10,11

Blessing   Pss. 23:2,3; 27:14; 28:8; 29:11; 31:24; 55:22; 105:4

Children of God   Deut. 14:1a; Matt. 13:43; Rom. 8:14; Gal. 4:7; Eph. 1:5; 1 John 3:2

Christ   John 13:13; Acts 2:36; Rom. 9:5; 1 Pet. 3:18; Rev. 1:7

Church   Matt. 16:18; 1 Cor. 3:9; Eph. 1:22,23; 5:23

Commitment   Ps. 37:4,5; Prov. 16:3

Communion   Matt. 26:28; John 6:51; 1 Cor. 10:16,17; 11:26

Eternal Life   1 John 5:13

Faith   Pss. 32:10; 40:4; Prov. 3:5; Matt. 21:22; Mark 9:23; 1 Cor. 2:5; Eph. 2:8; 1 Tim. 6:12; 1 John 5:4

Fear of God   Prov. 8:13; 9:10; 10:27

Fruit of the Spirit   Gal. 5:22,23

Glory of God   Ps. 97:6; 1 Cor. 10:31

Gospel   Mark 13:10

Grace   2 Cor. 4:15; Eph. 4:7; Heb. 4:16

Happiness   Pss. 144:15; 146:5; Prov. 16:20

Holiness   1 Cor. 15:34; 2 Cor. 7:1

Holy Spirit   John 14:16; Rom. 8:14; 1 Cor. 3:16; Gal. 4:6; 6:8; Eph. 3:16; 1 Thess. 5:19; 1 John 4:13

Instruction   Ps. 119:12; Prov. 23:21

Integrity   Prov. 3:3; 10:9; 12:22; 19:1; Luke 16:10; 1 Tim. 1:5

Joy   Pss. 5:11; 71:23; Phil. 4:4

Love   Ps. 116:1; Rom. 8:28,38,39; Eph. 5:2; 1 Thess. 3:12; 1 John 4:7,11,16,19

Missions   Ps. 96:3; Matt. 24:14; 28:19

Music   Pss. 98:4; 104:33

Obedience   John 14:15; 1 John 2:3

Peace   Matt. 5:9; Rom. 5:1; 8:6; Phil. 4:7; Col. 3:15

Praise   Pss. 47:6; 66:8

Prayer   Ps. 145:18; Isa. 65:24; Phil. 4:6; Col. 4:2; 1 Tim. 2:8; James 5:16

Repentance   Luke 5:32; 15:7

Resurrection   1 Cor. 6:14; Rev. 1:18

Sabbath   Ps. 118:24

Salvation   Isa. 12:2; John 1:12; 3:16; 14:6; Acts 4:12; 1 Thess. 5:9; Titus 3:5; 1 John 4:15

Scripture   2 Tim. 3:16,17

Servanthood   Matt. 20:26; John 12:26; Rom. 15:1; 2 Cor. 4:5; Gal. 6:10

Sin   Ps. 103:12; Isa. 1:18; Rom. 3:23; 6:23; 1 John 1:7

Truth   John 8:32

Word of God   Luke 16:17

Worship   Ps. 99:5; Luke 4:8; John 4:23

OTHER CLIP ART BOOKS FROM GOSPEL LIGHT

SON OF CLIP ART features over 1,000 drawings, borders, headers, Bible games (crosswords, mazes, etc.) and ideas to make great looking mailers and handouts for your youth program. This very popular resource is available at any Christian supply store, or use the handy order blank below.

THE SUNDAY SCHOOL CLIP ART BOOK

(Nursery through sixth grade) is an invaluable aid for putting together class worksheets, announcements to parents, and so on. Hundreds of illustrations, borders and designs by professional Christian artists.

The original **YOUTH WORKER'S CLIP ART BOOK** . . . the one that started it all! Complete your clip art resource library with this collection of the best artwork from Gospel Light's **LIGHT FORCE** creative team.

You can obtain these truly helpful resources at your local Christian supply store, or fill out and mail this order form:

Please check the box of each book you wish to receive.

1. ☐ *SON OF CLIP ART* (Youth) T5079 $14.95

2. ☐ *THE SUNDAY SCHOOL CLIP ART BOOK* (Children) T5081 $14.95

3. ☐ *THE YOUTH WORKER'S CLIP ART BOOK* (Youth) T5077 $14.95

☐ Please bill our church for cost plus shipping.
☐ I have enclosed a check for cost plus $2.00 shipping.

Your Name _____

Church Name _____

Church Address _____

City _____

State _____ Zip _____

Church Phone (____) _____

Total Sunday School Size _____

Mail this order form to:

**CLIP ART
P.O. Box 3875
Ventura, CA 93003**